Academic
Learning
Series

Microsoft®
Windows® 2000 Server

Lab Manual

PUBLISHED BY
Microsoft Press
A Division of Microsoft Corporation
One Microsoft Way
Redmond, Washington 98052-6399

Library of Congress Cataloging-in-Publication Data
MCSE Training Kit--Microsoft Windows 2000 Server / Microsoft Corporation.
     p. cm.
  Includes index.
  ISBN 1-57231-903-8
  ISBN 0-7356-0988-8 (Academic Learning Series)
  1. Electronic data processing personnel--Certification. 2. Microsoft
software--Examinations--Study guides. 3. Microsoft Windows 2000 server. I. Microsoft
Corporation.
  QA76.3 .M33455 2000
  005.7'13769--dc21   99-059501

Printed and bound in the United States of America.

4 5 6 7 8 9   QWTQWT   5 4 3 2 1

Distributed in Canada by Penguin Books Canada Limited.

A CIP catalogue record for this book is available from the British Library.

Microsoft Press books are available through booksellers and distributors worldwide. For further information about international editions, contact your local Microsoft Corporation office or contact Microsoft Press International directly at fax (425) 936-7329. Visit our Web site at mspress.microsoft.com. Send comments to *tkinput@microsoft.com*.

Acquisitions Editors: Anne Hamilton and Thomas Pohlmann
Project Editor: Julie Miller
Technical Editor: Steve Perry
Manuscript Editor: Melissa von Tschudi-Sutton

Authors: Bob Sheldon and Ethan Wilansky

Part No. 097-0002883

Introduction

This Lab Manual supplements the *ALS: Microsoft Windows 2000 Server* text-book. The labs in this manual are designed to be performed in a classroom by a group of students under the supervision of an instructor. This is in contrast to the hands-on exercises in the textbook, which are designed to be performed by individual students in an environment separate from the classroom. The labs in this manual and the hands-on exercises in the textbook form an essential part of your training because it is difficult to truly understand and use the operating system and its features without having first had the opportunity to explore the menus, options, and responses.

The labs in this manual do not precisely mirror the exercises in the textbook. Domain names, user names, IP addresses, shared resources, and other specific references in this manual are different than those in the textbook. Also, because it is not possible to predict each institution's local networking requirements, there might be slight differences between the names and addresses in your classroom and those appearing in these labs. Your instructor will explain any differences.

The labs are performed in a classroom that is set up as an isolated network. The instructor computer (named Instructor01) is a Microsoft Windows 2000 domain controller. The instructor computer includes shared folders that contain programs and data files that support the labs.

The old saying "The way to get to Carnegie Hall is to practice, practice, practice" is equally true of the pursuit of competence as you prepare for the Microsoft certification tests. The Microsoft Certified Professional (MCP) exams are demanding. One of the best ways to become confident in the use of Windows 2000 Server is to complete all the assigned labs in this manual as well as the hands-on exercises in the textbook.

Lab Navigation

The labs in this manual and the exercises in the textbook use drop-down menus to demonstrate how to navigate through Windows interface elements, such as Microsoft Management Console (MMC). There are rare instances when drop-down menus are not available, and in these cases, explicit instructions are provided for using context menus. You can activate an object's context menu by right-clicking the object.

The labs and textbook exercises use the Windows default double-click setting: double-click to open an item (single-click to select). Do not configure the computers to use the optional single-click to open an item (point to select) setting.

Lab 1: Exploring Microsoft Windows 2000 Server Features and Functions

Objectives

After completing this lab, you will be able to

- Describe many of the features in Windows 2000 Server.
- Explain how the Windows 2000 Server operating system supports Windows 16-bit and 32-bit applications.
- Show how the Windows 2000 operating system handles general protection faults and halted applications.

Estimated time to complete this lab: 40 minutes

Exercise 1
Exploring Windows 2000 Server Features

In this exercise, you will log on to the computer assigned to you by the instructor. You will then read about many of the features supported in Windows 2000 Server.

▶ **Logging on to the computer**

1. In the space provided, write down the domain user account name provided to you by the instructor.

   Domain user account name: Contoso_____

   The password for all student accounts is "password."

2. Start your computer.

3. When the Welcome To Windows screen appears, begin the logon process by pressing CTRL+ALT+DELETE.

   The Log On To Windows dialog box appears.

4. In the Log On To drop-down list, verify that Contoso appears.

   If you do not see the Log On To drop-down list, click the Options button.

5. In the User Name text box, type the student account name assigned to you by the instructor.

6. In the Password text box, type **password**.

7. Click OK.

   The Windows 2000 Configure Your Server screen appears.

▶ **Reading about Windows 2000 Server features**

1. Locate the Find Out What's New In Windows 2000 Server bullet item, and then click the What's New link.

   The Getting Started help file appears.

2. Use the table in the right pane to answer the following questions:

   What is the difference between removable storage and remote storage?

   Hint: Click the Disk And File Management Features link.

   _____

   _____

   _____

   _____

   _____

   _____

   What virtual private network (VPN) protocols are supported in Windows 2000 Server?

Hint: Click the Network Protocols And Technologies link.

_____

_____

_____

_____

_____

_____

What is the purpose of Microsoft IntelliMirror?

Hint: Click the IntelliMirror Features link.

_____

_____

_____

_____

_____

_____

_____

_____

3. Close the Getting Started help file.
4. On the left frame of the Windows 2000 Configure Your Server screen, click each of the following links and read about the corresponding features:

   Active Directory

   File Server

   Print Server

   Web/Media Server

   Networking

   Application Server

   Advanced

   Some of the links have subordinate links beneath them. Click these subordinate links as well and read about the corresponding features, but do not install or configure any services at this time.

5. When you are finished viewing Windows 2000 Server features, click the Home link in the left frame.

   The Configure Your Server screen appears.

6. Clear the Show This Screen At Startup check box.
7. Close the Windows 2000 Configure Your Server window.

Exercise 2
Exploring Operating System Functions

In this exercise, you will observe the ways in which Windows 16-bit and Windows 32-bit applications run in Windows 2000 and how they appear in Windows Task Manager.

▶ **Observing 16-bit and 32-bit applications in Windows Task Manager**

1. Click Start, and then click Run.

   The Run dialog box appears.

2. In the Open drop-down list, type **\\instructor01\students\labfiles\lab1**, and then click OK.

   The Lab1 window appears.

3. Double-click the following icons: Badapp32, Spind16, and Spind32.

   The Bad App, SpinDIB:32, and SpinDIB:16 applications appear.

4. Minimize the Lab1 window, and arrange the desktop so that you can see the three applications you started in the previous step.

5. In the SpinDIB:32 application, click the Open button.

   The Open dialog box appears.

6. Double-click the Mcsekit.bmp file icon.

   The Mcsekit.bmp image appears in the SpinDIB:32 window.

7. In the SpinDIB:16 application, click the Open button.

   The Open dialog box appears.

8. In the File Name text box, type **\\instructor01\students\labfiles\lab1\mcsekit.bmp**, and then click OK.

   The Mcsekit.bmp image appears in the SpinDIB:16 window.

9. Verify that the SpinDIB:32 and SpinDIB:16 applications are running by clicking the Spin! button in each application.

10. Click Start, and then click Run.

    The Run dialog box appears.

11. In the Open drop-down list, type **taskmgr**, and then click OK.

    The Windows Task Manager window appears.

    Four applications appear on the Applications tab: two SpinDB applications, Bad App, and Lab1 (the Lab1 window).

12. Open the Processes tab, and then scroll down to the bottom of the list.

    Many processes, including Badapp32.exe, Spind32.exe, and Spind16.exe appear in the list.

13. Why is Spind16.exe, along with Wowexec.exe, indented below Ntvdm.exe while Badapp32.exe and Spind32.exe are not?

   _____

   _____

   _____

   _____

   _____

   _____

   _____

   _____

14. Open the Applications tab.

15. In the Task column, right-click SpinDIB:16 - Mcsekit.bmp, and then click Go To Process.

   The Processes tab becomes active, and Spind16.exe is selected.

   The last two steps demonstrated that Spind16.exe is the active process of the SpinDIB:16 application.

16. Repeat the last two steps to complete the Process Name column of the following table:

Application name	Process name	Application type
SpinDIB:16	Spind16.exe	Windows 16-bit
Bad App	_____	Windows 32-bit
SpinDIB:32	_____	Windows 32-bit

17. Open the Processes tab.

18. On the Option menu, click Show 16-Bit Tasks to clear this option.

   The Spind16.exe process and the Wowexec.exe process disappear from the list on the Processes tab.

19. On the Option menu, click Show 16-Bit Tasks again so that 16-bit applications appear in the list on the Processes tab.

Exercise 3
Observing Halted Applications

In this exercise, you will test the effects of a halted 32-bit Windows application on other Windows applications. You will observe the result of a 16-bit Windows application that has caused a General Protection Fault (GPF), and then you will run the application again to observe the result of a hang. You will also observe the result of running 16-bit Windows applications in their own memory space.

▶   **Testing the effects of a halted 32-bit Windows application**

1. On the Options menu, click Always On Top to clear this option.

2. In the Bad App application, on the Action pull-down menu, click Hang.

    The fuse burns down, and the bomb explodes.

3. Move the mouse pointer over the Bad App window.

    The mouse pointer changes to an hourglass, demonstrating that Bad App is busy.

4. In Windows Task Manager, open the Applications tab.

    Bad App shows a status of Not Responding.

5. In the SpinDIB:32 and SpinDIB:16 windows, click the Flip! buttons.

    Why do both applications continue to respond normally even though the Bad App application is not responding?

    _____

    _____

6. In Windows Task Manager, verify that Bad App is selected, and then click the End Task button.

    The End Program - Bad App dialog box appears, warning you that ending the application this way will cause the loss of any unsaved data.

7. Click the End Now button.

    The Bad App application closes.

8. Leave the SpinDIB applications running, and continue to the next procedure.

▶   **Observing the results of GPF and halted applications**

1. Restore the Lab1 window, and double-click the Badapp16 icon.

    The Bad App application appears.

2. On the Action menu, click GP-Fault.

    When the fuse burns down, the bomb explodes and a Badapp message box appears, stating that an application error occurred.

3. Do not click the Close button or the Ignore button.

4. In the SpinDIB:32 window, click the Spin! button.

   The application responds to the spin request.

5. In the SpinDIB:16 window, click the Spin! button.

   The application does not respond.

6. In the Badapp message box, click the Close button.

   An Application Error message box appears.

7. Click the Close button.

8. In the SpinDIB:16 window, click the Spin! button.

   The application is now able to respond.

9. In the Lab1 window, double-click the Badapp16 icon again.

   The Bad App application appears.

10. On the Action menu, click Hang.

    When the fuse burns down, the bomb explodes and the application halts.

11. Move the mouse pointer over the SpinDIB:16 window.

    SpinDIB:16 does not respond.

12. Move the mouse pointer over the SpinDIB:32 window.

    The application is running normally.

13. Using Windows Task Manager, close Bad App.

14. Move the mouse pointer over the SpinDIB:16 window.

    The application is running normally.

15. After you halted Bad App, SpinDIB:16 was no longer responsive but
    SpinDIB:32 was. After you closed Bad App by using Windows Task Manager,
    SpinDIB:16 responded normally. Why did hanging Bad App affect
    SpinDIB:16 but not SpinDIB:32?

    _____

    _____

    _____

    _____

    _____

    _____

    _____

16. Leave the SpinDIB:16 and SpinDIB:32 windows open for the next procedure.

▶ **Running shared and exclusive Windows On Windows Virtual DOS Machines
(VDMs)**

1. Click Start, and then click Run.

   The Run dialog box appears.

2. In the Open drop-down list, type **cmd**, and then click OK.

   A command window appears.

3. At the command prompt, type **start /separate \\instructor01\students\
   labfiles\lab1\spind16.exe**, and then press ENTER.

4. In Windows Task Manager, open the Processes tab.

   A number of processes appear, including two ntvdm processes.

5. Why are there two ntvdm processes running?

   _____

   _____

   _____

   _____

6. Close the copy of SpinDIB:16 that you opened in step 3 of this procedure.

7. Close the command window.

8. Verify that the SpinDIB:16 and SpinDIB:32 applications you opened in Exercise 2 are still running.

9. Restore the Lab1 window.

10. Select the Spind16 icon.

11. On the File menu, click Create Shortcut.

    A Shortcut message box appears, stating that a shortcut cannot be created in the Lab1 window but it can be created on the desktop.

Note You cannot create a shortcut in the Lab1 window because your student account does not have write access to this folder.

---

12. Click the Yes button.

    The Shortcut To Spind16 icon appears on the desktop.

13. Right-click the Shortcut To Spind16 icon, and then click Properties.

    The Shortcut To Spind16 Properties dialog box appears, and the Shortcut tab is active.

14. Select the Run In Separate Memory Space check box and the Run As Different User check box, and then click OK.

15. Double-click the Shortcut To Spind16 icon.

    The Run As Other User dialog box appears.

16. Why did this dialog box appear?

    _____

    _____

    _____

    _____

    _____

17. Select the Run The Program As Contoso\Student*xx* radio button, and then click OK.

18. Verify that two ntvdm processes appear in Windows Task Manager.

19. In the Lab1 window, double-click the Badapp16 icon.

    The Bad App application appears.

20. On the Action menu, click Hang.

    The fuse burns down, and the bomb explodes.

21. Check the status of both running copies of SpinDIB:16.

22. Why is one copy of SpinDIB:16 not responding while the other is?

    _____

    _____

    _____

    _____

23. In Windows Task Manager, close Bad App.

24. Close Windows Task Manager, the SpinDIB applications, and the Lab1 window.

Lab 2: Installing Microsoft Windows 2000 Server

Objectives

After completing this lab, you will be able to

- Describe the three phases (Pre-Copy, Text Mode, and GUI Mode) of the installation process for Windows 2000 Server.
- Perform a new installation of Windows 2000 Server as a stand-alone server.

Estimated time to complete this lab: 40 minutes

Exercise 1
Installing and Configuring Windows 2000 Server

You will complete this exercise on your student computer. It is assumed for this procedure that the student computer is already running Windows 2000 Server configured by a lab administrator.

▶ **Running the Pre-Copy phase of Windows 2000 Server Setup**

1. In the space provided, write down the computer name provided to you by the instructor.

   Computer name:_____

2. Log on to your computer with your assigned student ID and password.

3. Click Start, and then click Run.

   The Run dialog box appears.

4. In the Open drop-down list, type **\\instructor01\windist\winnt32 /s:\\instructor01\windist /tempdrive:d**, and then click OK.

Note It is not necessary to enter any switches in the previous command. However, installation is partially automated by adding the /s and /tempdrive switches. For more information on these switches, refer to the textbook or type **\\instructor01\windist\winnt32 /?** at the command prompt.

The Welcome To The Windows 2000 Setup Wizard screen appears, prompting you to upgrade or install a new copy of Microsoft Windows 2000.

5. Select the Install A New Copy Of Windows 2000 (Clean Install) radio button, and then click Next.

   The License Agreement screen appears.

6. Select the I Accept This Agreement radio button, and then click Next.

   The Your Product Key screen appears.

7. Type the product key provided by the instructor, and then click Next.

   The Select Special Options screen appears.

8. Verify that your language options are correct, and then click Next.

   A Please Wait screen appears briefly, and then the Directory Of Applications For Windows 2000 screen appears.

9. Click Next.

   The Copying Installation Files screen appears. This copy process can take a while to complete. Eventually, the Restarting The Computer screen appears for 15 seconds, and then the computer restarts.

▶ **Running the Text Mode phase of Windows 2000 Server Setup**

After the computer restarts, the Microsoft Windows 2000 Server Setup option is automatically selected on the boot menu, and then the Text Mode phase of Setup begins. A gray bar at the bottom of the screen indicates that the computer is being inspected and that the Windows 2000 Executive is loading. If you are installing the evaluation version of Windows 2000, a setup notification screen appears, informing you that you are about to install a time-limited evaluation version of Windows 2000.

1. Press ENTER.

   The Welcome To Setup screen appears. You are then informed that the existing installation can be repaired, a new installation can continue, or the installation process can be aborted.

2. Press ENTER.

   The existing copy of Windows 2000 Server is detected.

3. Press ESC to continue the new installation.

   The Windows 2000 Server Setup screen appears, prompting you to select an area of free space in which to install Windows 2000, to create a partition, or to delete a partition.

4. Verify that D: NTFS is selected, and then press ENTER.

   After disk examination, files are copied to the installation folders. This may take several minutes. The setup process counts down for 15 seconds and then restarts the computer.

▶ **Running the GUI Mode phase of Windows 2000 Server Setup**

A Windows 2000 Setup message box appears, followed by the Welcome To The Windows 2000 Server Setup Wizard screen. This is the beginning of the graphical portion of Setup.

Note You do not need to click Next; the installation will automatically proceed to the Installing Devices screen.

---

1. On the Regional Settings screen, make sure that the system locale, user locale, and keyboard layout are correct for your language and location, and then click Next.

   The Personalize Your Software screen appears, prompting you for your name and the name of your organization.

2. In the Name text box, type **student**; in the Organization text box, type the name of your organization; and then click Next.

   The Licensing Modes screen appears, prompting you to select a licensing mode. By default, the Per Server radio button is selected.

3. Select the Per Seat radio button, and then click Next.

The Computer Name And Administrator Password screen appears.

4. In the Computer Name text box, type **srvdc***xx* (where *xx* is the two-digit number assigned to you by the instructor).

Windows 2000 displays the computer name in all capital letters regardless of how it is entered.

5. In the Administrator Password text box and the Confirm Password text box, type **student** (all lowercase), and then click Next.

The Windows 2000 Components screen appears.

6. Click Next.

If a modem is detected in the computer during setup, the Modem Dialing Information screen appears.

7. If the Modem Dialing Information screen appears, enter an area code or city code, and then click Next.

The Date And Time Settings screen appears.

8. Enter the correct date, time, and time zone settings, and then click Next.

Important Windows 2000 services perform tasks that depend on the computer's time and date settings. Please be sure to select the correct settings for your location to avoid problems in later labs.

The Networking Settings screen appears, and networking components are installed.

▶ **Installing and configuring Windows networking components**

In this procedure, you will configure basic networking.

1. On the Networking Settings screen, verify that the Typical Settings radio button is selected, and then click Next.

The Workgroup Or Computer Domain screen appears, prompting you to join either a workgroup or a domain.

2. Verify that the No, This Computer Is Not On A Network, Or Is On A Network Without A Domain radio button is selected and that the workgroup name is Workgroup, and then click Next.

After a brief pause, the Installing Components screen appears. Then, the Performing Final Tasks screen appears, which shows the status as the setup process continues. Computers that do not exceed the minimum hardware requirements may take 30 minutes or more to complete this phase of the installation.

The Completing The Windows 2000 Setup Wizard screen appears.

3. Click the Finish button.

Windows 2000 restarts and runs the newly installed copy of Windows 2000 Server.

Note You will see two listings for Windows 2000 Server on the boot menu. The first listing is the stand-alone server you just installed. The second listing is the member server used to complete Lab 1.

4. At the completion of the startup phase, begin the logon process by pressing CTRL+ALT+DELETE.

   The Log On To Windows dialog box appears.

5. In the User Name text box, verify that Administrator appears, and in the Password text box, type **student**.

6. Click OK.

   If Windows 2000 detects hardware that was not detected earlier in the setup process, the Found New Hardware Wizard screen appears, indicating that Windows 2000 is installing drivers.

7. If the Found New Hardware Wizard screen appears, verify that the Restart The Computer When I Click Finish check box is cleared, and then click Finish to complete the hardware driver installation process.

   The Windows 2000 Configure Your Server screen appears.

8. Select the I Will Configure This Server Later radio button, and then click Next.

9. Clear the Show This Screen At Startup check box.

10. Close the Windows 2000 Configure Your Server window.

▶   **Performing basic configuration of Windows 2000 Server**

In this procedure, you adjust display properties and customize the appearance of the boot menu.

1. Write down the following video configuration settings provided to you by the instructor:

   Colors:_____

   Screen Area:_____

   Refresh Frequency:_____

Warning If the instructor cannot provide you with the refresh frequency that the monitor supports, do not change the default setting. Setting the refresh frequency too high might damage the monitor.

2. Click Start, point to Settings, and then click Control Panel.

   Control Panel appears.

3. Double-click the Display icon.

The Display Properties dialog box appears.

Note The Display Properties dialog box is also accessible from the Desktop context menu. Context menus are not being used in this lab manual unless there is no easy alternative navigation procedure.

4. Open the Settings tab. Adjust the settings in the Colors and Screen Area sections according to the values provided by the instructor.

5. Click the Advanced button.

The Properties dialog box for the video adapter and monitor appears.

6. Open the Monitor tab, and verify that the value in the Refresh Frequency drop-down list matches the value provided by the instructor.

7. Click OK.

A monitor and video adapter message box appears, warning you that your settings will be applied and that if you don't respond, the original display settings will be restored.

8. Click OK.

If the display settings are valid, a Monitor Settings message box appears.

9. Click the Yes button to make the changes permanent.

10. Click OK to close the Display Properties dialog box.

11. Close Control Panel.

12. Click Start, and then click Run.

The Run dialog box appears.

13. In the Open drop-down list, type **cmd**, and then click OK.

A command window appears.

14. At the command prompt, type **c:**, and then press ENTER.

15. Type **attrib boot.ini -h -s**, and then press ENTER.

The attrib command line in this step removes the hidden and system attributes from the Boot.ini file so that you can edit the file.

16. Type **notepad boot.ini**, and then press ENTER.

Microsoft Notepad is launched, and the contents of the Boot.ini file are displayed.

17. Locate the [operating systems] section.

18. Change the part of the first line under the [operating systems] section in quotes from "Microsoft Windows 2000 Server" to "Srvdc*xx*" (where *xx* is the two-digit number assigned to you by the instructor).

19. Change the part of the second line under the [operating systems] section in quotes from "Microsoft Windows 2000 Server" to "Server*xx*" (where *xx* is the two-digit number assigned to you by the instructor).

Warning Do not modify the ARC path information preceding the text in quotation marks or the switches following the text in quotation marks.

---

20. On the File menu, click Exit.

    A Notepad message box appears, asking if you want to save the changes to Boot.ini.

21. Click the Yes button.

    Notepad closes.

22. Close the command window.

23. Shut down and restart the computer.

    After the computer finishes its POST routine, notice that the boot menu options have changed.

24. Press ENTER to run the copy of Windows 2000 Server you installed in this lab.

Lab 3: Preparing an Automated Installation of Microsoft Windows 2000 Server

Objectives

After completing this lab, you will be able to

- Run Setup Manager.
- Inspect the distribution folder.
- Customize Setup.
- Run an unattended installation.

Estimated time to complete this lab: 40 minutes

Exercise 1
Preparing and Running an Automated Installation

In this exercise, you will install and run Setup Manager to create an answer file and a local distribution of the setup files. Then you will perform an unattended installation of Windows 2000 Server.

▶ **Running Setup Manager**

1. Log on as Administrator with a password of "student."

2. Make a folder named Deploy underneath D:\Program Files.

3. Click Start, and then click Run.

   The Run dialog box appears.

4. In the Open drop-down list, type **\\instructor01\students\labfiles\lab3\ support\tools**, and then click OK.

   The Enter Network Password dialog box appears.

5. In the Connect As text box, type **studentxx** (where *xx* is your assigned two-digit number).

6. In the Password text box, type **password**, and then click OK.

7. The Tools window appears.

8. Double-click the Deploy icon.

   The Deploy window appears.

9. On the Edit menu, click Select All.

10. On the File menu, click Extract.

    A Browse For Folder dialog box appears.

11. Expand the New Volume (D:) node.

12. Expand the Program Files node.

13. Select the Deploy folder, and then click OK.

    The files in the Deploy cabinet file are extracted to D:\Program Files\Deploy.

14. Close the Deploy window.

15. On the desktop, double-click the My Computer icon, and then double-click the New Volume (D:) icon.

16. Double-click the Program Files folder.

    The Program Files window appears and its contents are hidden.

17. Click the Show Files link.

    Folders appear.

18. Double-click the Deploy folder.

    The Deploy window appears.

19. Double-click the Setupmgr icon.

    The Microsoft Windows 2000 Setup Manager wizard appears.

20. Read the descriptive text, and then click Next.

    The New Or Existing Answer File screen appears with the Create A New Answer File radio button selected.

21. Click Next.

    The Product To Install screen appears with the Windows 2000 Unattended Installation radio button selected.

22. Click Next.

    The Platform screen appears with the Windows 2000 Professional radio button selected.

23. Select the Windows 2000 Server radio button, and then click Next.

    The User Interaction Level screen appears with the Provide Defaults radio button selected.

24. Select each radio button, and read the text appearing in the Description box.

25. Select the Fully Automated radio button, and then click Next.

    The License Agreement screen appears.

26. Read the text on this screen, select the I Accept The Terms Of The License Agreement check box, and then click Next.

    The Customize The Software screen appears.

27. In the Name text box, type your name.

28. In the Organization text box, type your organization name, and then click Next.

    The Licensing Mode screen appears with the Per Server radio button selected.

29. Select the Per Seat radio button, and then click Next.

    The Computer Names screen appears.

30. In the Computer Name text box, type **srvsa**xx (where xx is the two-digit number assigned to you by the instructor).

31. Click the Add button.

    The Computers To Be Installed list box contains the computer name entered in the previous step.

32. Click Next.

    The Administrator Password screen appears.

33. In the password text boxes, type **password**, and then select the When The Computer Starts, Automatically Log On As Administrator check box.

    The Number Of Times To Auto Logon spin box is set to 1.

34. Click Next.

    The Display Settings screen appears.

35. Leave all text box values set to the Use Windows Default option, and then click Next.

    The Network Settings screen appears, and the Typical Settings radio button is selected.

36. Click Next.

    The Workgroup Or Domain screen appears with the Workgroup radio button selected.

    Srvdc*xx* is currently configured as a member of a workgroup named Workgroup. Do not change the values appearing on the Workgroup Or Domain screen. When the automated installation is run on this computer, the new installation of Microsoft Windows 2000 Server will become a member of the same workgroup. Later in your training, Srvdc*xx* will become a domain controller. The installation for which you are now preparing an answer file will remain a stand-alone server.

Note The answer file can be modified to automatically join a domain and create computer accounts in the domain. These modifications are made by using either Setup Manager or a text editor.

---

37. Click Next.

    The Time Zone screen appears.

38. From the Time Zone drop-down list, select your time zone, and then click Next.

    The Additional Settings screen appears with the Yes, Edit The Additional Settings radio button selected.

39. Click Next.

    The Telephony screen appears.

40. Click Next.

    The Regional Settings screen appears with the Use The Default Regional Settings For The Windows Version You Are Installing radio button selected.

41. Click Next.

    The Languages screen appears.

42. In the Language Groups list, select any additional language support you want to have available for the operation of Windows 2000 Server, and then click Next.

    The Browser And Shell Settings screen appears with the Use Default Internet Explorer Settings radio button selected.

43. Click Next.

    The Installation Folder screen appears with the A Folder Named Winnt radio button selected.

44. Select the This Folder radio button, and then type **Win2kSA**.

45. Click Next.

    The Install Printers screen appears.

46. In the Network Printer Name text box, type **\\instructor01\LJ5**, and then click the Add button.

47. Click Next.

    The Run Once screen appears.

48. In the Command To Run text box, type **notepad.exe**, and then click the Add button.

    Typically, the Command To Run text box contains a script or other executable program to further configure the user's environment. For the purpose of training, running Notepad is sufficient. Notice that the AddPrinter command runs to add the network printer to the list of installed printers.

49. Click Next.

    The Distribution Folder screen appears.

50. Select the Yes, Create Or Modify A Distribution Folder radio button, and then click Next.

    The Distribution Folder Name screen appears with the Create A New Distribution Folder radio button selected.

    The Distribution Folder text box contains D:\Win2000dist, and the Share As text box contains Win2000dist.

51. Click Next.

    The Additional Mass Storage Drivers screen appears.

52. Read the screen, and then click Next.

    The Hardware Abstraction Layer screen appears.

53. Read the screen, and then click Next.

    The Additional Commands screen appears.

54. Read the screen, and then click Next.

    Commands entered here are written to the Cmdlines.txt file, which is created under the distribution folder in the OEM subfolder.

    The OEM Branding screen appears.

55. Click Next.

    The Additional Files Or Folders screen appears.

56. Browse the folders by clicking them and reading the information that appears in the Description box.

57. Click Next.

    The Answer File Name screen appears.

58. Verify that the Location And File Name text box displays D:\Win2000dist\Unattend.txt, and then click Next.

    The Location Of Setup Files screen appears.

59. Select the Copy The Files From This Location radio button, and in the text box, type **\\instructor01\windist**.

60. Click Next.

    The Copying Files screen appears as the files are copied from the instructor computer to the D:\Win2000dist folder on the student computer.

61. Allow the file copy to complete before continuing to the next procedure.

    At the completion of Setup Manager's tasks, a Completing The Windows 2000 Setup Manager Wizard screen appears.

62. Read the screen, and then click the Finish button.

63. Close the Deploy window.

▶ **Inspecting the distribution folder created by Setup Manager and customizing Setup**

In this procedure, you inspect the folder structure and files created by Setup Manager and edit the answer file (Unattend.txt) and batch file (Unattend.bat) to further automate the setup process.

1. Click Start, and then click Run.

    The Run dialog box appears.

2. In the Open drop-down list, type **d:\win2000dist**, and then click OK.

    The Win2000dist window appears.

3. Open a window to \\Instructor01\WinDist.

4. Arrange the windows so that you can see both the Win2000dist window and the Windist On Instructor01 window.

5. What folder appears in the Win2000dist window that does not appear in the Windist On Instructor01 window?

    _____

6. Examine the folder structure below OEM, and review Figure 3.1 in the *ALS: Microsoft Windows 2000 Server* textbook to verify that they are the same.

7. Click the Back button on the toolbar.

    The Win2000dist window appears.

8. In the Win2000dist window, locate the two Unattend files.

Note If you create an answer file for multiple computers, a .UDF file also appears in the distribution folder. If the answer file is named Unattend.txt, the UDF file is named Unattend.udf.

The Unattend files do not appear with extensions.

9. To show file extensions for all files, on the Tools menu, click Folder Options.

   The Folder Options dialog box appears.

10. Open the View tab.

11. In the Advanced Settings list, clear the Hide File Extensions For Known File Types check box, and then click OK.

12. Locate the Unattend files again.

   The Unattend files appear with their file extensions showing.

13. Double-click the Unattend.txt file.

   Notepad is launched, and the contents of the Unattend.txt file are displayed.

14. Review the contents of the Unattend.txt file.

15. Click Start, and then click Run.

   The Run dialog box appears.

16. In the Open drop-down list, type **d:\program files\deploy\unattend.doc**, and then click OK.

   Microsoft Wordpad is launched, and the contents of the Unattend.doc file are displayed.

17. Locate and read about the ProductID key.

18. Close Unattend.doc.

19. Click the Notepad window so that it has the focus.

20. Locate the [User Data] section.

21. As the last entry in the [User Data] section, type **ProductID=*instructor provided product id***, where *instructor provided product id* is a number provided by the instructor.

22. Save and close Unattend.txt.

23. What is the purpose of the .UDF file?

   Hint: You created an answer file for a single computer. As a result, an Unattend.udf file was not created.

---

24. In the Win2000dist window, select Unattend.bat.

25. On the File menu, click Edit.

   Notepad is launched, and the contents of the Unattend.bat file are displayed.

26. Append the /tempdrive:d switch to the last command line in Unattend.bat so that the command is changed to \\srvdcxx\win2000dist\winnt32 /s:%SetupFiles% /unattend:%AnswerFile% /tempdrive:d.

   Notice that the batch file sets variables, and then the variables are used to run Winnt32 with switches.

Note If a multiple computer answer file is created, the computer name is added when running the batch file because a .UDF file is called during the setup routine.

---

27. Save and close Unattend.bat.

28. Close the Win2000dist window and the Windist On Instructor01 window.

▶ **Running an unattended setup of Windows 2000 Server**

In this procedure, you will run the unattended installation you created and customized in the previous procedures.

1. Open a command window, and go to the D: prompt.

2. Type **cd win2000dist**, and then press ENTER.

3. Type **unattend**, and then press ENTER.

4. The Copying Installation Files screen appears as Windows 2000 Server runs an automated installation.

   At the conclusion of this phase, a Restarting The Computer screen appears, informing you that the computer is about to be restarted.

Note This pre–Text Mode phase of Setup can be completed by using the /syspart switch with Winnt32.exe.

---

5. Allow the computer to restart.

   The Windows 2000 boot menu appears, and Setup continues to the Text Mode phase.

   The computer reboots again, and the boot menu appears showing Microsoft Windows 2000 Server and the other operating systems installed.

   Windows 2000 installation continues with the GUI Mode phase of Setup. The Installing Devices and Installing Components screens take time to complete. The Performing Final Tasks screen appears when Windows 2000 Server completes the setup routine. When the setup process is complete, the Windows 2000 Setup screen announces that the computer will restart.

6. After the computer restarts, notice that it automatically logs on as Administrator (specified in Setup Manager). At this point, the printer is installed and Notepad runs.

   The Windows 2000 Configure Your Server screen appears.

7. Select the I Will Configure This Server Later radio button, and then click Next.

   The Configure Your Server screen appears.

8. Clear the Show This Screen At Startup check box, and then close the screen.

9. In order to save space for labs occurring later in this course, delete the D:\Win2000dist folder.

10. Customize the Boot.ini file so that the new listing named Microsoft Windows 2000 Server is changed to Srvsa*xx* (where *xx* is the two-digit number assigned to you by the instructor).

    If you are not sure how to perform this task, refer to Lab 2.

11. Open Control Panel, and then double-click the System icon.

    The System Properties dialog box appears.

12. Open the Advanced tab, and then click the Startup And Recovery button.

    The Startup And Recovery dialog box appears.

13. In the Default Operating System drop-down list, select "Srvdc*xx*" /Fastdetect.

14. Change the Display List Of Operating Systems For spin box to 5 seconds, and then click OK.

    The System Properties dialog box appears.

15. Click OK.

16. Close Control Panel.

17. Open the Printers window to verify that the HP LaserJet 5 On instructor01 icon appears.

18. Close the Printers window.

19. Shut down the computer.

Lab 4: Installing File Transfer Protocol (FTP) and Configuring the Hard Disk

Objectives

After completing this lab, you will be able to

- Install FTP on a computer running Windows 2000 Server.
- Create and configure a primary partition.
- Create and configure an extended partition, and then create logical drives.

Estimated time to complete this lab: 25 minutes

Exercise 1
Installing FTP and Configuring the Hard Disk

In this exercise, you will install FTP Server on Srvdc*xx*. Then you will create multiple primary partitions and an extended partition in the unallocated portion of Disk 0.

▶ **Installing FTP**

1. Click Start, point to Programs, point to Accessories, and then click Command Prompt.

    The Command Prompt window appears.

2. At the command prompt, type **net use * \\instructor01\windist /user:student*xx* password**, and then press ENTER.

    A connection is established to Instructor01, and the connection is assigned a drive letter.

3. Close the Command Prompt window.

4. Click Start, point to Settings, and then click Control Panel.

    Control Panel appears.

5. Double-click the Add/Remove Programs icon.

    The Add/Remove Programs window appears.

6. In the left pane, click Add/Remove Windows Components.

    The Windows Components wizard appears.

7. In the Components list, click Internet Information Services (IIS), and then click the Details button.

    The Internet Information Services (IIS) dialog box appears.

8. In the Subcomponents Of Internet Information Services (IIS) list, select the File Transfer Protocol (FTP) Server check box.

9. Click OK.

10. Click Next.

    The Configuring Components screen appears as the configuration changes are made. After a few minutes, the Files Needed dialog box appears.

11. Verify that \\Instructor01\Windist appears in the Copy Files From text box, and then click OK.

12. If the Files Needed dialog box appears again, repeat step 11.

13. When the Completing The Windows Components Wizard screen appears, click the Finish button.

14. Click the Close button to close the Add/Remove Programs window.

15. Close Control Panel.

16. Double-click the My Computer icon on your desktop.

    The My Computer window appears.

17. Click the icon that links to the \\Instructor01\WinDist network share.

18. On the File menu, click Disconnect.

    The icon to the \\Instructor01\WinDist network share is removed from the My Computer window.

19. Close the My Computer window.

▶   **Configuring a simple disk and converting it to a dynamic disk**

1. Click Start, point to Programs, point to Administrative Tools, and then click Computer Management.

   The Computer Management snap-in appears.

2. In the left pane, expand the Storage node if it is not already expanded, and then select the Disk Management node.

Note If the Write Signature And Upgrade Disk wizard appears when you click the Disk Management node, close the wizard and proceed with the following steps.

The Volume List window (top) and the Graphical View window (bottom) appear in the right pane. Notice that Disk 0 has two primary partitions (C: and D:) and some unallocated disk space.

3. Select the unallocated space in the Graphical View window.

4. On the Action menu, point to All Tasks, and then click Create Partition.

   The Create Partition wizard appears.

5. Read the information on the Welcome To The Create Partition Wizard screen, and then click Next.

   The Select Partition Type screen appears.

6. Verify that the Primary Partition radio button is selected, and then click Next.

   The Specify Partition Size screen appears.

7. In the Amount Of Disk Space To Use text box, type **100**, and then click Next.

   The Assign Drive Letter Or Path screen appears.

8. Select H: from the Assign A Drive Letter drop-down list, and then click Next.

   The Format Partition screen appears.

9. Verify that the Format This Partition With The Following Settings radio button is selected, select the Perform A Quick Format check box, and then click Next.

   The Completing The Create Partition Wizard screen appears.

10. Review the information on the screen, and then click the Finish button.

    After Windows 2000 Server has completed the create partition request, an H: partition will appear in the Graphical View window.

11. If a System Change message box appears asking you to restart your computer, click the Yes button to restart the computer. Once the restart is complete, log on to the computer again as Administrator with a password of "student."

12. Following the previous steps in this procedure, create an extended partition in the remaining unallocated disk space on Disk 0.

13. Review the settings for drive H: in the Volume View window. Notice that the free space appearing in the Graphic View window does not contain any drive letters. This area is the extended partition in which you will assign logical drives.

14. In the Graphical View window, select the Free Space box in the extended partition.

15. On the Action menu, point to All Tasks, and then click Create Logical Drive.

    The Create Partition wizard appears.

16. Read the information on the Welcome To The Create Partition Wizard screen, and then click Next.

    The Select Partition Type screen appears.

17. Verify that the Logical Drive radio button is selected, and then click Next.

    The Specify Partition Size screen appears.

18. In the Amount Of Disk Space To Use text box, type **150**, and then click Next.

    The Assign Drive Letter Or Path screen appears.

19. Select the Mount This Volume At An Empty Folder That Supports Drive Paths radio button, and then click the Browse button.

    The Browse For Drive Path dialog box appears.

20. Expand the D: node, and then expand the Inetpub node.

21. Select the Ftproot node, and then click OK.

    The Mount This Volume At An Empty Folder That Supports Drive Paths text box shows the path D:\Inetpub\Ftproot.

22. Click Next.

    The Format Partition screen appears.

23. Select the Perform A Quick Format check box, and select the Enable File And Folder Compression check box. Verify that NTFS appears in the File System To Use drop-down list. In the Volume Label text box, delete any existing text and type **FTPVol**.

24. Click Next.

    The Completing The Create Partition Wizard screen appears.

25. Review the information on the screen, and then click the Finish button.

    Notice that because this procedure did not ask that you specify volume names, the H: partition shows the volume name of New Volume (H:).

26. To change the volume name, select New Volume (H:) in the Volume View window or the Graphical View window.

27. On the Action menu, point to All Tasks, and then click Properties.

    The New Volume (H:) Properties dialog box appears.

28. In the Label text box, delete New Volume, and then click OK.

    Your disk configuration for Disk 0 should now be as follows:

Drive/Path	Format	Partition Type	Purpose
C:	NTFS	Primary	System
D:	NTFS	Primary	Boot
H:	NTFS	Primary	Unused
FTPVol	NTFS	Extended	Files saved to D:\InetPub \Ftproot are redirected to this disk partition.
N/A	N/A	Extended	Free space. (The amount of free space will vary based on the size of Disk 0.)

29. To check that FTPVol is a partition available to D:\Inetpub\Ftproot, open Windows Explorer.

30. In the left pane, expand the My Computer node, expand the (D:) node, and then expand the Inetpub node.

    Notice that the Ftproot node appears as a drive icon. Any files stored on D:\Inetpub\Ftproot are redirected to the FTPVol in the extended partition.

31. Close Windows Explorer, and close the Computer Management snap-in.

Lab 5: Configuring Distributed File System (Dfs)

Objectives

After completing this lab, you will be able to

- Create folders and shares.
- Create a stand-alone Dfs root.
- Create Dfs links.
- Create a Dfs replica.

Estimated time to complete this lab: 25 minutes

Exercise 1
Creating a Dfs Root and a Dfs Link

In this exercise, you will first create the necessary folders to support the Dfs roots and links. You will then share those folders. From there, you will create a stand-alone Dfs root and Dfs links, and then create a Dfs replica. Finally, you will access files through the Dfs structure.

▶ **Creating directories and shares**

In this procedure, you create or use existing folders and create shares for the folders. You can use any method you prefer to create folders and shares or follow the steps in this procedure.

1. Log on to Srvdc*xx* as Administrator with a password of "student."
2. Open My Computer, and then open Local Disk (H:).
3. On the File menu, point to New, and then click Folder.

   A folder named New Folder appears in the Local Disk (H:) window, and the blinking cursor appears inside the icon's label text box.
4. Rename the folder "Public," and then press ENTER or click outside of the text box.
5. Select the Public folder, and on the File menu, click Sharing.

   The Public Properties dialog box appears.
6. Select the Share This Folder radio button, and in the Comment text box, type **dfs root share**.
7. Click OK.

   The Public folder appears with a hand beneath the folder.
8. Create the folders and shares listed in the following table.

Drive	Folder	Share name	Purpose/Comment
C:	\Inetpub\Wwwroot	Internal	Internal Web content
H:	\Press	Press	Current press releases
D:	\Inetpub\Ftproot	Ftproot	FTP root directory mapped partition
H:	\Dev\TechDocs	TechDocs	Technical documents area
D:	\Public\Press	PressRepl	Current press releases replica

▶ **Creating a stand-alone Dfs root on Srvdc*xx***

In this procedure, you create a stand-alone Dfs root to host the shares created in the last procedure.

1. Click Start, point to Programs, point to Administrative Tools, and then click Distributed File System.

   The Distributed File System snap-in appears.

2. Read the message displayed in the right pane.

3. On the Action menu, click New Dfs Root.

   The New DFS Root wizard appears.

4. Read the information on the Welcome To The New Dfs Root Wizard screen, and then click Next.

   The Select The Dfs Root Type screen appears.

5. Notice that there are two types of Dfs roots that you can create:

   a. A domain Dfs root that writes the Dfs tree topology to the Active Directory store and supports Domain Name System (DNS), multiple levels of Dfs links, and file replication.

   b. A stand-alone Dfs root that does not use the Active Directory store and that permits a single level of Dfs links.

   Because you have not configured a domain controller at this point in your training, you will create a stand-alone Dfs root.

6. Select the Create A Standalone Dfs Root radio button, and then click Next.

   The Specify The Host Server For The Dfs Root screen appears.

7. Confirm that Srvdc*xx* is displayed in the Server Name text box, and then click Next.

   The Specify The Dfs Root Share screen appears.

8. Notice that you can use an existing share for the Dfs root, or the wizard can create a new shared folder for you.

9. Verify that the Use An Existing Share radio button is selected, and then in the drop-down list, select Public.

10. Click Next.

    The Name The Dfs Root screen appears.

11. In the Comment text box, type **public access share**, and then click Next.

    The Completing The New Dfs Root Wizard screen appears.

12. Review the settings on the screen, and then click the Finish button.

    The Dfs root is added to the Distributed File System snap-in.

► **Creating Dfs links**

In this procedure, you will create Dfs links below the \\Srvdc*xx*\Public Dfs root.

1. In the left pane of the Distributed File System snap-in, select \\Srvdc*xx*\Public.

2. Click the Action menu, and notice that the New Root Replica command and the Replication Policy command are not available.

3. On the Action menu, click New Dfs Link.

   The Create A New Dfs Link dialog box appears.

4. In the Link Name text box, type **Intranet**.

5. Click the Browse button.

   The Browse For Folder dialog box appears.

6. Navigate to the Srvdc*xx* node.

7. Expand the Srvdc*xx* node, select the Internal node, and then click OK.

   The Send The User To This Shared Folder text box now contains \\Srvdc*xx*\Internal.

8. In the Comment text box, type **internal web content**, and then click OK.

9. Create additional Dfs links by using information in the following table. Always begin the process of creating a link by selecting \\Srvdc*xx*\Public in the Distributed File System snap-in.

Link name	Send the user to this shared folder	Comment
News	\\Srvdc*xx*\Press	Current press releases
FTP	\\Srvdc*xx*\Ftproot	FTP root directory
Tech	\\Srvdc*xx*\TechDocs	Technical documents area

Note Rather than browsing for a share, you can enter the server and share name by using standard universal naming convention (UNC) syntax.

▶ **Creating a Dfs replica**

In this procedure, you create a replica of the News Dfs link. This Dfs link points to the H:\Press folder, which is shared as Press. The replica will be stored in the D:\Public\Press folder, which is shared as PressRepl.

Note Because you created a stand-alone Dfs link, files must be manually copied or synchronized between the two folders. File replication services are not available for replicas created on a stand-alone Dfs link.

1. Select the News Dfs link in the left pane of the Distributed File System snap-in.

2. On the Action menu, click New Replica.

   The Add A New Replica dialog box appears.

3. In the Send The User To This Shared Folder text box, type **\\srvdc*xx*\pressrepl**. Notice that no replication policy can be configured for this replica.

4. Click OK.

   In the right pane, both the \\Srvdc*xx*\Press share and the \\Srvdc*xx*\PressRepl share appear.

▶ **Accessing Dfs on Srvdc*xx***

In this procedure, you will use the batch file provided with this course to copy files to Dfs links created in the previous procedures. After the files are copied, you will access the files through Windows Explorer.

1. Click Start, point to Programs, point to Accessories, and then click Command Prompt.

   The Command Prompt window appears.

2. At the command prompt, type **net use * \\instructor01\students /user:student*xx* password**, and then press ENTER.

   A connection is established to Instructor01, and the connection is assigned a drive letter.

3. Close the Command Prompt window.

4. Copy the Lab5copy.bat file from the \\Instructor01\Students\Labfiles\Lab5 folder to the D:\Documents and Settings\Administrator\My Documents folder on Srvdc*xx*.

5. Disconnect your connection to the Instructor01 computer.

6. Double-click the Lab5copy.bat icon in the D:\Documents And Settings\Administrator\My Documents folder.

   A command window will open as files are copied to the Dfs links, and then the command window will close.

7. Click Start, and then click Run. In the Open drop-down list, type **\\srvdc*xx*\public**, and then click OK.

   The Public window appears. The four Dfs links that you created in the previous procedures appear in the window.

8. Open each folder, and verify that the following files are present:

Folder	File(s)
FTP	Dirmap.htm, Dirmap.txt
Intranet	Compaq.html, Q240126 - Best Practices For Using Sysprep With NTFS Volumes.htm
News	Press.wri
Tech	Dfsnew.doc, RFS 1777.txt

Note that the Intranet folder will contain additional files since this folder points to a folder created during the installation of Windows 2000 Server.

9. Which previously empty folder represents a mounted drive?

_____

_____

10. Earlier in this exercise, you created a replica of the News Dfs link. The name of that replica is \\Srvdc*xx*\PressRepl. This replica is a shared folder by the name of PressRepl and is located in D:\Public\Press. If you examine the contents of this folder, you will notice that it is empty. However, when you view the News Dfs link, you will notice that there is a file named Press.wri. Why is the PressRepl Dfs replica empty?

_____

_____

_____

_____

_____

_____

Tip You can use the Distributed File System snap-in to check the status of a Dfs link and to open a window to the contents of the link.

11. Close the Public window.

Lab 6: Installing and Configuring Active Directory Services, Dfs, and the Administrative Tools Package

Objectives

After completing this lab, you will be able to

- Install Active Directory services.
- Install the Administrative Tools package (Adminpak.msi).
- Change from stand-alone Dfs to domain Dfs.
- Create an organizational unit and its objects.
- Manage Active Directory objects.

Estimated time to complete this lab: 90 minutes

Exercise 1
Installing Active Directory Services

In this exercise, you will install DNS and promote your stand-alone server, Srvdc*xx*, to a domain controller, a process that includes installing Active Directory services. In addition, you will create a child domain of the Contoso domain.

▶ **Installing DNS on your stand-alone server**

1. Start Srvdc*xx*, and log on as Administrator with a password of "student."

2. If the Windows 2000 Configure Your Server screen appears, close it.

3. Click Start, point to Programs, point to Accessories, and then click Command Prompt.

   The Command Prompt window appears.

4. At the command prompt, type **net use * \\instructor01\windist /user:studentxx password**, and then press ENTER.

   A connection is established to Instructor01, and the connection is assigned a drive letter.

5. Close the Command Prompt window.

6. Click Start, point to Settings, and then click Control Panel.

   The Control Panel window appears.

7. Double-click the Add/Remove Programs icon.

   The Add/Remove Programs window appears.

8. In the left pane, click the Add/Remove Windows Components button.

   The Windows Components wizard appears.

9. In the Components list, select Networking Services, and then click the Details button.

   The Networking Services dialog box appears.

10. In the Subcomponents Of Networking Services list, select the Domain Name System (DNS) check box.

11. Click OK.

12. Click Next.

    The Configuring Components screen appears as the configuration changes that you specified are made. After a few minutes, the Optional Networking Components message box appears, telling you that the computer has a dynamically assigned IP address.

Note If the Files Needed dialog box appears, change the path to *drive:*, where *drive* is the drive letter that was mapped to \\Instructor01\Windist in step 4 of this procedure.

---

13. Click OK.

    The Local Area Connection Properties dialog box appears.

14. Select Internet Protocol (TCP/IP), and then click the Properties button.

    The Internet Protocol (TCP/IP) Properties dialog box appears.

15. Select the Use The Following IP Address radio button.

16. In the IP Address text box, type **10.1.10.xx**, where *xx* is the two-digit number in your computer name and user name. If the first digit in your two-digit number is 0, Windows 2000 will automatically drop the 0 when you click OK.

17. Tab to the Subnet Mask text box, and verify that a default subnet mask of 255.0.0.0 is automatically entered into the text box.

18. Verify that the Use The Following DNS Server Addresses radio button is selected.

19. In the Preferred DNS Server text box, type **10.1.10.xx**, the IP address of your computer.

20. In the Alternate DNS Server text box, type **10.1.1.1**, the IP address of the Instructor01 computer.

21. Click OK.

22. Click OK to close the Local Area Connection Properties dialog box.

    The Completing The Windows Components Wizard screen appears.

23. Click the Finish button.

24. Close the Add/Remove Programs window.

25. Close Control Panel.

26. Disconnect your \\Instructor01\Windist network drive.

▶ **Promoting a stand-alone server to a domain controller**

In this procedure, you run Dcpromo.exe to install Active Directory services on your stand-alone server, making it a domain controller in a new child domain.

1. Click Start, and then click Run.

2. In the Open text box, type **dcpromo.exe**, and then click OK.

    The Active Directory Installation wizard appears.

3. Click Next.

    The Domain Controller Type screen appears.

4. Verify that the Domain Controller For A New Domain radio button is selected, and then click Next.

    The Create Tree Or Child Domain screen appears.

5. Select the Create A New Child Domain In An Existing Domain Tree radio button, and then click Next.

   The Network Credentials screen appears.

6. In the User Name text box, type **administrator**.

7. In the Password text box, type **password**.

8. In the Domain text box, type **contoso**.

9. Click Next.

   The Child Domain Installation screen appears.

10. Click the Browse button.

    The Browse For Domain dialog box appears.

11. Select Contoso.msft, and then click OK.

12. In the Child Domain text box, type **Domainxx**, where *xx* matches the two-digit number in your computer name and user ID. Notice that the complete DNS name of the new domain appears in the Complete DNS Name Of New Domain text box.

13. Click Next.

    The NetBIOS Domain Name screen appears.

14. Verify that Domain*xx* appears in the Domain NetBIOS Name text box, and then click Next.

    The Database And Log Locations screen appears.

15. Verify that D:\Winnt\Ntds is the location of both the database and the log, and then click Next.

    The Shared System Volume screen appears.

16. Read the information on the screen, and then verify that the Sysvol folder location is D:\Winnt\Sysvol.

17. Click Next.

    The Permissions screen appears.

18. Verify that the Permissions Compatible With Pre-Windows 2000 Servers radio button is selected, and then click Next.

    The Directory Services Restore Mode Administrator Password screen appears.

19. Read this screen, type **student** in both text boxes, and then click Next.

    The Summary screen appears, listing the options you selected.

20. Review the contents of the screen, and then click Next.

    The Configuring Active Directory progress indicator appears as Active Directory services is installed on the server. When the process has completed, the Completing The Active Directory Installation Wizard screen appears.

21. Click the Finish button.

    The Active Directory Installation Wizard dialog box appears.

22. Click the Restart Now button.

    It will take longer than usual for Windows 2000 Server to start the first time as a domain controller.

► **Adding a domain user account to the local domain**

In this procedure, you add a user account that exists in the Contoso domain to the Domain*xx* local domain.

1. On Srvdc*xx*, log on to Domain*xx* as Administrator with a password of "student."

2. Click Start, point to Programs, point to Administrative Tools, and then click Active Directory Users And Computers.

    The Active Directory Users And Computers snap-in appears.

3. In the console tree, select the Builtin node.

    A list of built-in user groups appears in the right pane.

4. Double-click Administrators.

    The Administrators Properties dialog box appears.

5. Open the Members tab, and then click the Add button.

    The Select Users, Contacts, Computers, Or Groups dialog box appears.

6. In the Look In drop-down list, select Contoso.msft.

7. From the list of users, contacts, computers, and groups, select Student *xx* (Student*xx*@Contoso.msft).

8. Click the Add button.

    The user account is added to the box below.

9. Click OK.

    The user account is added to the Members list in the Administrators Properties dialog box.

10. Click OK again.

11. Close the Active Directory Users And Computers snap-in.

12. Click Start, and then click Shut Down.

    The Shut Down Windows dialog box appears.

13. Select Log Off Administrator, and then click OK.

▶ **Viewing your domain**

1. On Srvdc*xx*, log on to the Contoso domain as Student*xx* with a password of "password."

2. Double-click the My Network Places icon on your desktop.

    The My Network Places window appears.

3. Double-click the Entire Network icon, and then click the Entire Contents link.

4. Double-click the Microsoft Windows Network icon.

    Notice that icons for the Contoso and Domain*xx* domains appear.

5. Close the Microsoft Windows Network window.

▶ **Using Active Directory Users And Computers to view your domain**

1. Click Start, point to Programs, point to Administrative Tools, and then click Active Directory Users And Computers.

    The Active Directory Users And Computers snap-in appears.

2. On the Action menu, click Connect To Domain.

    The Connect To Domain dialog box appears.

3. Click the Browse button.

    The Browse For Domain dialog box appears.

4. Expand the Contoso.msft node, and then select the Domain*xx*.Contoso.msft node.

5. Click OK.

    Your domain appears in the Domain text box.

6. Select the Save This Domain Setting For The Current Console check box.

7. Click OK.

8. Notice that Domain*xx*.Contoso.msft replaced Contoso.msft in the console tree.

9. In the console tree, expand the Domain*xx*.Contoso.msft node.

10. Examine each of the nodes below Domain*xx*.Contoso.msft. Do not modify any information that you see in these nodes.

11. What selections are listed under Domain*xx*.Contoso.msft and what is the purpose of each of these items? Hint: you can find a description for many of these nodes by examining their properties.

_____

_____

_____

_____

_____

_____

_____

_____

_____

12. Close the Active Directory Users And Computers snap-in.

Exercise 2
Installing and Examining the Contents of the Administrative Tools Package (Adminpak.msi)

In this exercise, you will first list the tools that appear on the Administrative Tools menu. Then you will install the Administrative Tools package (Adminpak.msi) and notice the additional tools that appear on the menu.

▶ **Adjusting Start menu settings and reviewing new tools installed under Administrative Tools**

In this procedure, you disable the feature that shows only the most used items on the Start menu.

1. On Srvdc*xx*, log on to the Contoso domain as Student*xx* with a password of "password."

2. Click Start, point to Settings, and then click Taskbar & Start Menu.

    The Taskbar And Start Menu Properties dialog box appears.

3. Clear the Use Personalized Menus check box, and then click OK.

4. Click Start, point to Programs, and then point to Administrative Tools.

    When Srvdc*xx* was a stand-alone server, fewer applications appeared under Administrative Tools. Tools specific to Active Directory services, domains, and DNS maintenance have been added. For each tool in the list below, place the mouse pointer over the name of the tool on the Administrative Tools submenu and read the tool tip. Write the purpose of each tool below its name in the list.

    Active Directory Domains And Trusts

    _____

    _____

    Active Directory Sites And Services

    _____

    _____

    Active Directory Users And Computers

    _____

    _____

    DNS

    _____

    _____

▶ **Installing additional administration tools**

In this procedure, you install the Windows 2000 Administrative Pack. These tools can also be installed on Microsoft Windows 2000 Professional to facilitate remote administration of Windows 2000 Servers.

1. Click Start, and then click Run.

   The Run dialog box appears.

2. In the Open drop-down list, type **adminpak.msi**.

   Adminpak.msi is located in the D:\Winnt\System32 folder, which is in the search path. Therefore, there is no need to type the path to this Microsoft installer file.

3. Click OK.

   The Windows 2000 Administration Tools Setup wizard appears.

4. Read the information on the screen, and then click Next.

   The Setup Options screen appears.

5. Select the Install All Of The Administrative Tools radio button, and then click Next.

   The Installation Progress screen appears as the administrative tools are installed. When the installation is complete, the Completing The Windows 2000 Administration Tools Setup Wizard screen appears.

6. Click the Finish button.

   Notice that additional tools have been installed on the Start menu under Administrative Tools. To determine the purpose of each tool, place the mouse pointer over each new tool and a tool tip will appear.

Exercise 3
Changing from a Stand-Alone Dfs to a Domain Dfs

In Lab 4, you installed a stand-alone Dfs root. In this exercise, you will delete the stand-alone Dfs root and create a domain Dfs root.

▶ **Deleting the stand-alone Dfs root**

Only one Dfs root can exist on a server. Therefore, the stand-alone Dfs must first be deleted on Srvdc*xx* before you can create the domain Dfs root.

1. Click Start, point to Programs, point to Administrative Tools, and then click Distributed File System.

   The Distributed File System snap-in appears.

2. In the console tree, select the \\Srvdc*xx*\Public node.

3. On the Action menu, click Delete Dfs Root.

   A Distributed File System message box appears stating that deleting the Dfs root disables the ability to access the Dfs again. This procedure does not delete the shares that were linked to the Dfs root.

4. Click the Yes button.

▶ **Creating a domain Dfs**

The domain Dfs will be configured similarly to the stand-alone Dfs, but it will provide file replication to the Dfs link replicas.

1. In the console tree of the Distributed File System snap-in, select the Distributed File System node.

2. On the Action menu, click New Dfs Root.

   The New Dfs Root wizard appears.

3. Click Next.

   The Select The Dfs Root Type screen appears.

4. Verify that the Create A Domain Dfs Root radio button is selected, and then click Next.

   The Select The Host Domain For The Dfs Root screen appears. Domain*xx*.Contoso.msft appears in the Domain Name text box, and Contoso.msft and Domain*xx*.Contoso.msft appear in the Trusting Domains text box.

5. Click Next.

   The Specify The Host Server For The Dfs Root screen appears.

   Notice that Srvdc*xx*.Domain*xx*.Contoso.msft is shown in the Server Name text box. If Srvdc*xx* were still hosting the stand-alone Dfs, its name would not be written in the Server Name text box. This is intentional because a server can host only one Dfs root.

6. Click Next.

The Specify The Dfs Root Share screen appears.

7. Verify that the Use An Existing Share radio button is selected, and then select Public in the drop-down list.

8. Click Next.

The Name The Dfs Root screen appears.

9. In the Comment text box, type **Public access share**, and then click Next.

10. The Completing The New Dfs Root Wizard screen appears.

11. Review the settings on the screen. Notice that the host server is Srvdc*xx*.Domain*xx*.Contoso.msft. When you created a stand-alone Dfs root, the host server name was Srvdc*xx*.

12. Click the Finish button.

The new Dfs root is added to the console tree in the Distributed File System snap-in.

▶   **Creating Dfs links**

In this procedure, you re-create the Dfs links that you created in Lab 4.

1. In the console tree of the Distributed File System snap-in, select the \\Domain*xx*.Contoso.msft\Public node.

The \\Srvdc*xx*\Public Dfs root appears in the right pane.

2. Click the Action menu, and notice that the New Root Replica command is available. Now that Active Directory services has been installed and the server has been set up as a domain controller, you can create Dfs root replicas and Dfs link replicas.

3. On the Action menu, click New Dfs Link.

The Create A New Dfs Link dialog box appears.

4. In the Link Name text box, type **Intranet**.

5. In the Send The User To This Shared Folder text box, type **\\srvdc*xx*\internal**.

6. In the Comment text box, type **Internal web content**, and then click OK.

7. Create three more new Dfs links by using information in the following table.

Link name	Send the user to this shared folder	Comment
News	\\Srvdc*xx*\Press	Current press releases
FTP	\\Srvdc*xx*\Ftproot	FTP root directory
Tech	\\Srvdc*xx*\TechDocs	Technical documents area

Exercise 4
Creating an Organizational Unit and Its Objects

In this exercise, you will create part of the organizational structure of a domain by creating an organizational unit (OU). You then create three user accounts for use in a later exercise.

▶   **Creating OUs and user objects**

1. On Srvdc*xx*, log on to the Contoso domain as Student*xx* with a password of "password."

2. Open the Active Directory Users And Computers snap-in.

3. In the console tree, select the Domain*xx*.Contoso.msft node.

4. On the Action menu, point to New, and then click Organizational Unit.

   The New Object - Organizational Unit dialog box appears.

   Notice that the only required information is the name. The dialog box indicates the location where the object will be created. This should be Domain*xx*.Contoso.msft.

5. In the Name text box, type **Sales**, and then click OK.

   The Sales OU appears in the console tree.

6. Under Domain*xx*.Contoso.msft, create another OU named Servers.

7. In the console tree, select the Users node.

8. On the Action menu, point to New, and then click User.

   The New Object - User dialog box appears.

Note User objects can be created in any OU. In this procedure, however, you will create most user objects in the Users OU.

---

9. In the First Name text box, type **Jane**.

10. In the Last Name text box, type **Doe**.

11. In the User Logon Name text box, type **Jane Doe**.

12. Click Next.

13. The next New Object - User dialog box appears.

14. Leave the password fields blank, and do not change the default settings for this user account.

15. Click Next.

    The summary screen appears showing the full name and user logon name for Jane Doe.

16. Click the Finish button.

17. Click Jane Doe in the right pane of the Active Directory Users And Computers snap-in.

18. On the Action menu, click Properties.

   The Jane Doe Properties dialog box appears.

19. On the General tab, type **555-1234** in the Telephone Number text box.

20. Click OK.

21. Create the following user accounts in the Users organizational unit.

Text box	Information to type
First name	**John**
Last name	**Smith**
User logon name	**John_Smith**

Text box	Information to type
First name	**Bob**
Last name	**Train**
User logon name	**Bob_Train**

You will be working with these user accounts in Lab 7.

Exercise 5
Managing Active Directory Objects

In this exercise, you will first search for a user object that you created in the last exercise and then move the object to a new location.

▶ **Finding a user account in the domain**

In this procedure, you locate a user with a first name of Jane. Jane was promoted to a position in the sales department, so her user object will be moved to the Sales OU. You know most of her telephone number, and you know her first name.

1. On Srvdc*xx*, log on to the Contoso domain as Student*xx* with a password of "password."

2. Open the Active Directory Users And Computers snap-in.

3. In the console tree, select the Domain*xx*.Contoso.msft node.

4. On the Action menu, click Find.

   The Find Users, Contacts, And Groups dialog box appears.

5. Verify that Users, Contacts, And Groups is selected in the Find drop-down list, and then click Find Now.

   Notice how all users and groups are located, regardless of their location.

6. Click Clear All.

   The Find In The Directory message box appears.

7. Click OK to acknowledge that you want to clear the search results.

8. In the In drop-down list, verify that Domain*xx* appears.

9. In the Name text box, type **Jane**.

10. Open the Advanced tab.

11. Click Field, point to User, and then click Telephone Number.

Note If you don't see Telephone Number listed, click the arrow at the bottom of the list to scroll down to that command.

   Verify that Starts With appears in the Condition text box.

12. In the Value text box, type **555**, and then click the Add button.

13. Click Find Now.

   A results pane is added to the bottom of the Find Users, Contacts, And Groups dialog box.

You can modify the information that is displayed in the search results by clicking Choose Columns on the View menu and adding and removing columns.

14. Close the Find Users, Contacts, And Groups dialog box.

▶   **Moving an object in Active Directory Users And Computers**

1. In the console tree of the Active Directory Users And Computers snap-in, select the Users node.

   A list of user and group objects appears in the right pane.

2. Select the Jane Doe user object in the right pane.

3. On the Action menu, click Move.

   The Move dialog box appears.

4. Select the Sales node, and then click OK.

   Jane Doe is moved from the Users OU to the Sales OU.

5. In the console tree, select the Sales node.

   The Jane Doe user object appears in the right pane.

Lab 7: Administering Microsoft Windows 2000 Server

Objectives

After completing this lab, you will be able to

- Navigate and create a custom Microsoft Management Console (MMC) console.
- Modify domain user account properties.
- Create a roaming profile and assign a home folder.
- Change the domain mode.
- Create groups.
- Create a group policy object and set a policy.
- Modify software policies.

Estimated time to complete this lab: 90 minutes

Exercise 1
Navigating an MMC Console and Creating a Custom MMC Console

In this exercise, you use one of the MMC consoles included with Windows 2000 Server and then create a customized MMC console.

▶ **Using an existing MMC console**

1. On Srvdc*xx*, log on to the Contoso domain as Student*xx* with a password of "password."

2. Click Start, point to Programs, point to Administrative Tools, and then click Event Viewer.

   The Event Viewer snap-in appears, giving you access to the contents of the event log files on your computer. You can use the Event Viewer snap-in to monitor various hardware and software activities.

   Notice that a number of logs are listed. The logs that always appear when Windows 2000 Server is installed are the Application log, Security log, and System log. Additional logs appear as additional services are added. Event Viewer should also be showing the Directory Service log, because your server is configured to run Active Directory services; a DNS Server log, because it is configured to run as a DNS server; and a File Replication Service log, because it is running FRS.

3. Close the Event Viewer snap-in.

▶ **Creating and manipulating a customized MMC console**

Next you will create a customized MMC console and use it to confirm the last time your computer was started. You also add a snap-in with extensions.

1. Click Start, and then click Run.

   The Run dialog box appears.

2. In the Open drop-down list, type **mmc**, and then click OK.

   MMC starts and displays an empty console.

3. Maximize the Console1 and Console Root windows.

4. On the Console menu, click Options to view the currently configured options.

   The Options dialog box appears.

5. In what mode is the console running?

   _____

   _____

6. Verify that Author Mode appears in the Console Mode drop-down list, and then click OK.

7. On the Console menu, click the Save button.

The Save As dialog box appears.

Notice that the default location for customized consoles is the Administrative Tools folder, which maps to the Administrative Tools Program Group for the currently logged on user. You can see the file structure by clicking the down arrow in the Save In drop-down list.

8. In the File Name text box, type **All Events**, and then click the Save button.

   The name of your console appears in the MMC window title bar.

9. On the Console menu, click Exit.

10. Click Start, point to Programs, point to Administrative Tools, and then click All Events.

    The All Events console appears.

11. On the Console menu, click Add/Remove Snap-In.

    The Add/Remove Snap-In dialog box appears with the Standalone tab active. Notice there are currently no loaded snap-ins.

12. Click the Add button.

    The Add Standalone Snap-In dialog box appears.

13. Select Event Viewer, and then click the Add button.

    The Select Computer dialog box appears, allowing you to specify which computer you want to administer.

    Notice that you can add the Event Viewer snap-in for the local computer you are working on, or if your local computer is part of a network, you can also add the Event Viewer snap-in for a remote computer.

14. Verify that the Local Computer: (The Computer This Console Is Running On) radio button is selected, and then click the Finish button.

15. In the Add Standalone Snap-In dialog box, click the Close button.

16. In the Add/Remove Snap-In dialog box, click OK.

    Event Viewer (Local) now appears in the console tree.

Tip If you cannot view the entire name of a node on the console tree, drag the border between the console panes to the right.

---

17. Expand the Event Viewer (Local) node, and then click System.

    The most recent system events are shown in the right pane.

18. Double-click the most recent event listed as Information in the Type column and as Eventlog in the Source column.

    The Event Properties dialog box appears, showing that the Event Log service was started as part of your system startup. The date and time represents the approximate time your system was started.

19. Click OK.

20. On the Console menu, click Exit.

    A Microsoft Management Console dialog box appears, asking if you want to save the console settings.

21. Click the No button.

22. Click Start, and then click Run.

    The Run dialog box appears.

23. In the Open drop-down list, type **mmc**, and then click OK.

24. Maximize the Console1 and Console Root windows.

25. On the Console menu, click Add/Remove Snap-In.

    The Add/Remove Snap-In dialog box appears with the Standalone tab active.

26. Click the Add button.

    The Add Standalone Snap-In dialog box appears.

27. Click Computer Management, and then click the Add button.

    The Computer Management dialog box appears.

28. Verify that the Local Computer: (The Computer This Console Is Running On) radio button is selected, and then click the Finish button.

29. Click the Close button.

    Computer Management (Local) appears in the list of snap-ins that have been added.

30. In the Add/Remove Snap-In dialog box, click OK.

    Computer Management (Local) appears under Console Root.

31. Expand the Computer Management (Local) node, review the available functions, and then expand the System Tools node.

Note Do not use any of the tools at this point.

Notice that several extensions are available, including Device Manager and System Information. You can restrict the functionality of a snap-in by removing extensions.

32. On the Console menu, click Add/Remove Snap-In.

    The Add/Remove Snap-In dialog box appears.

33. Click Computer Management (Local), and then open the Extensions tab.

    A list of extensions available to the Computer Management snap-in appears.

34. Clear the Add All Extensions check box, and then in the Available Extensions list, clear the Device Manager Extension check box and the System Information Extension check box.

35. Click OK.

36. In the console tree, expand the Computer Management (Local) node, and then expand the System Tools node to confirm that the Device Manager extension and the System Information extension were removed.

Note Do not use any of the tools at this point.

---

37. On the Console menu, click Options.

    The Options dialog box appears.

38. From the Console Mode drop-down list, select User Mode - Limited Access, Single Window.

39. Select the Do Not Save Changes To This Console check box, and then click OK.

40. Close the console.

    A Microsoft Management Console dialog box appears.

41. Click the Yes button.

    The Save As dialog box appears.

42. In the File Name text box, type **ComputerMmgmt Restricted**, and then click the Save button.

43. Click Start, point to Programs, point to Administrative Tools, and then click ComputerMgmt Restricted.

    Notice that the custom console opens in a single window.

44. Close the custom console.

Exercise 2
Modifying Domain User Account Properties

In Lab 6, you created three user accounts. In this exercise, you will use the Active Directory Users And Computers snap-in to manipulate the properties of the Jane Doe, John Smith, and Bob Train user accounts.

▶   **Manipulating user accounts**

In this procedure, you modify the user accounts you created in the previous lab by configuring the Logon Hours, Account Expiration, and Password Restriction settings. You add these user accounts to the Print Operators group so that the users can log on locally to the domain controller. You then test the Logon Hours, Account Expiration, and Password Restriction settings.

1. On Srvdc*xx*, log on to the Contoso domain as Student*xx* with a password of "password."

2. Click Start, point to Programs, point to Administrative Tools, and then click Active Directory Users And Computers.

   The Active Directory Users And Computers snap-in appears.

3. Expand the Domain*xx*.Contoso.msft node in the left pane if it is not already expanded.

4. Select the Users node.

5. In the Details pane, double-click Bob Train.

   The Bob Train Properties dialog box appears with the General tab active.

   Notice that on the General tab, you specify a number of user account properties in addition to first and last name. Properties such as Office and Telephone Number are especially useful for locating users.

6. Open the Account tab, and then click the Logon Hours button.

   The Logon Hours For Bob Train dialog box appears.

   Notice that Bob Train is permitted to log on at any time.

7. To restrict Bob Train's logon hours, locate the current day of the week and select a three-hour block of time starting with the current time.

Important You must complete this entire exercise in the next three hours for this account restriction to work properly. Otherwise, extend the account restriction to the time when you plan to complete the exercise.

A frame outlines the blocks for all the selected hours, and the time restriction appears at the bottom of the dialog box.

8. Select the Logon Denied radio button.

The outlined area is now a white block, indicating that the user will not be permitted to log on during those hours.

Tip To select the same block of time for all days in the week, in the All row, click the gray block that represents the start time, and then drag the pointer to the end time. To select an entire day, click the gray block that is labeled with the name of the day.

9. Click OK.

10. In the Bob Train Properties dialog box, click OK to apply your settings and close the dialog box.

11. In the Details pane of the Active Directory Users And Computers snap-in, double-click John Smith.

   The John Smith Properties dialog box appears with the General tab active.

12. Open the Account tab.

13. When will the account expire?

   _____

   _____

   _____

14. In the Account Expires group, select the End Of radio button, and then set the date to today's date.

15. Click OK.

16. In the console tree, select the Sales node.

   The Jane Doe account appears in the Details pane.

17. Double-click Jane Doe.

   The Jane Doe Properties dialog box appears with the General tab active.

18. Open the Account tab.

19. In the Account Options list, select the User Must Change Password At Next Logon check box.

20. Click OK.

21. Close the Active Directory Users And Computers snap-in.

22. Click Start, and then click Shut Down.

   The Shut Down Windows dialog box appears.

23. Select Log Off Student*xx* from the drop-down list, and then click OK.

   Windows 2000 logs off the Student*xx* account and displays the Welcome To Windows message box.

▶   **Attempting to log on with a user account**

1. Log on to Domain*xx* as Jane_Doe with no password.

   The Logon Message warning box appears, indicating that your password has expired and must be changed.

2. Click OK.

   The Change Password dialog box appears, and the cursor is in the Old Password text box.

3. Press the TAB key, because the Jane Doe account was not assigned a password.

4. In the New Password and Confirm New Password text boxes, type **student**, and then click OK.

   The Change Password message box appears, indicating that your password was changed.

5. Click OK.

   Were you able to log on successfully? Why or why not?

   _____

   _____

   _____

   _____

6. Click OK to close the Logon Message message box.

▶   **Granting local logon access to user accounts**

There are several ways to allow regular users to log on locally at a domain controller. In this procedure, you add the three users you created in the previous lab to the Print Operators group, because this group has the right to log on to a domain controller.

Note A group is a collection of user accounts. Groups simplify administration by allowing you to assign rights and permissions to a group of users rather than having to assign rights and permissions to each individual user account. You will learn more about groups later in this lab.

---

1. Log on to the Contoso domain as Student*xx* with a password of "password."

2. Open Active Directory Users And Computers, and in the console tree, select the Sales node.

3. In the Details pane, double-click Jane Doe.

   The Jane Doe Properties dialog box appears.

4. Open the Member Of tab.

5. Click the Add button.

   The Select Groups dialog box appears.

6. In the list of groups, select Print Operators, and then click the Add button.

7. The Print Operators group is added to the large text box at the bottom of the dialog box.

8. Click OK.

9. Click OK again to close the Jane Doe Properties dialog box.

   In the next steps, you will use a simpler method to add both the Bob Train and John Smith accounts to the Print Operators group.

10. In the console tree, select the Users node.

11. In the Details pane, select Bob Train, press and hold down the CTRL key, and click John Smith.

12. On the Action menu, click Add Members To A Group.

    The Select Group dialog box appears.

13. In the list of groups, double-click Print Operators.

    An Active Directory message box appears, stating that the Add To Group operation completed successfully.

14. Click OK.

15. Close the Active Directory Users And Computers snap-in, and then log off the computer.

16. Attempt to log on to Domainxx as Jane_Doe with a password of "student."

    Notice that you are now able to log on locally with the Jane Doe user account.

17. Attempt to log on to Domainxx as Bob_Train with no password.

    Notice that you were not able to log on because of an account restriction. In the first procedure of this exercise, you restricted Bob Train's logon hours.

18. Attempt to log on to Domainxx as John_Smith with no password.

    Notice that you are allowed to log on. In the first procedure of this exercise, you set John Smith's account expiration to the end of the day. If you try to log on as John_Smith tomorrow, logon will fail because of an account restriction.

19. Log off of Srvdcxx.

Exercise 3
Creating a Roaming Profile and Assigning a Home Folder

In this exercise, you use the Jane Doe user account to create a profile. You log on as Jane_Doe to create a local profile for the account, and then log on as Student*xx* and use the System utility in Control Panel to verify that the profile for Jane Doe was created. Later, you create and test a home folder for Jane Doe.

▶   **Creating a user profile template**

In this procedure, you define and test a local user profile. Typically, a computer running Windows 2000 Professional would be used to create a user profile template. However, in this case, you will use Windows 2000 Server.

1. Log on to Domain*xx* as Jane_Doe with a password of "student."

   The first time that you logged on to the computer using the Jane Doe account, a local user profile was created for her with default settings. This local profile will be customized and then assigned to other users.

2. On the desktop, Double-click the My Computer icon.

   The My Computer window appears.

3. Drag the Local Disk (C:) icon to the desktop.

   A Shortcut message box appears stating that this item cannot be copied or moved but a shortcut can be created.

4. Click the Yes button to create a shortcut to the C: drive.

5. Close the My Computer window.

6. Click Start, point to Settings, and then click Control Panel. In the Control Panel window, double-click the Display icon.

   The Display Properties dialog box appears.

7. Open the Appearance tab.

   Notice the current color scheme.

8. In the Scheme drop-down list, select a different color scheme, and then click OK.

   The desktop changes to the new color scheme.

9. Close the Control Panel window.

10. Log off Jane_Doe, and then log on to the Contoso domain as Student*xx* with a password of "password."

11. Open Control Panel, and then double-click the System icon.

    The System Properties dialog box appears.

12. Open the User Profiles tab.

Notice that there are multiple user profiles, some in the Contoso domain and some in the Domain*xx* domain. These profiles represent all user accounts that have logged on to the two domains.

13. Do not close the System Properties dialog box because you will need it to complete the next procedure.

▶ **Defining and assigning a mandatory roaming profile**

1. On the D: drive of computer Srvdc*xx*, create a folder named Profiles.

2. Share the new folder as Profiles.

3. Open the Profiles folder, and create a subfolder named Shared.

    Close the Profiles window.

4. Activate the System Properties dialog box that you opened previously.

5. Open the User Profiles tab if it is not already active.

6. In the Profiles Stored On This Computer list, select Domain*xx*\Jane_Doe, and then click the Copy To button.

    The Copy To dialog box appears.

7. In the Copy Profile To text box, type **d:\profiles\shared**.

8. In the Permitted To Use group, click the Change button.

    The Select User Or Group dialog box appears.

9. In the Look In drop-down list, select Domain*xx*.Contoso.msft.

10. In the list of users and groups, select Users, and then click OK.

    Builtin\Users appears in the Permitted To Use section.

11. Click OK to return to the System Properties dialog box.

    A Confirm Copy message box appears, stating that the D:\Profiles\Shared folder already exists and that the current contents will be deleted. This appears because you already created the folder for the profile.

12. Click the Yes button.

13. Click OK to close the System Properties dialog box.

14. Open the Active Directory Users And Computers snap-in.

15. Expand the Domain*xx*.Contoso.msft node if it is not already expanded, and then select the Users node.

16. In the Details pane, double-click John Smith.

    The John Smith Properties dialog box appears.

17. In an earlier exercise, you set an account expiration for the John Smith account. To remove this expiration, open the Account tab, and select the Never radio button in the Account Expires group.

18. Open the Profile tab.

19. In the Profile Path text box, type **\\srvdcxx\profiles\shared**, and then click OK.

    Close the Active Directory Users And Computers snap-in.

    Because you are using a centralized profile that could be assigned to other users, the next step is to configure the profile as mandatory.

20. Open the D:\Profiles\Shared folder.

    Notice that user profile folders appear.

21. On the Tools menu, click Folder Options.

    The Folder Options dialog box appears.

22. Open the View tab.

23. Select the Show Hidden Files And Folders radio button, and clear the Hide File Extensions For Known File Types check box.

24. Click OK.

    The Shared window now shows hidden files and folders. Notice that the Ntuser.dat file appears.

25. Select the Ntuser.dat icon.

26. On the File menu, click Rename.

    The file name box is selected and can be edited.

27. Change the extension so that the file name is Ntuser.man, and then press ENTER.

28. Close the Shared window.

29. Log off Student*xx* and log on to Domain*xx* as John_Smith with no password.

    The John Smith desktop appears. Notice that the John Smith user is using the color scheme you assigned to the user profile template and the Shortcut to Local Disk (C:) icon appears on the desktop.

30. To test the mandatory profile, delete the Connect To The Internet icon on the desktop.

31. Log off and log on again to Domain*xx* as John_Smith with no password.

    Notice that the Connect To The Internet icon appears on the desktop. This happens because you assigned a mandatory profile to the John Smith user account.

▶   **Assigning a home folder to a user**

1. Log off John_Smith and log on to the Contoso domain as Student*xx* with a password of "password."

2. Create a folder on the D: drive named HomeDirs.

3. Share this folder as HomeDirs.

4. Open the Active Directory User And Computers snap-in.

5. Open the John Smith Properties dialog box, and then open the Profile tab.

6. In the Home Folder group, select the Connect radio button.

7. Verify that Z: appears in the Connect drop-down list.

8. In the To text box, type **\\srvdcxx\homedirs\%username%**, and then click OK.

9. Close the Active Directory Users And Computers snap-in.

10. Select the HomeDirs folder in the D: window.

11. On the File menu, click Properties.

   The HomeDirs Properties dialog box appears.

12. Open the Security tab.

   Notice that the Everyone group is granted Full Control permission for this directory.

13. Click the Add button.

   The Select Users, Computers, Or Groups dialog box appears.

14. In the list of groups, select the Users group, and then click the Add button.

15. Click OK.

   The Users group is added to the list of names on the Security tab of the HomeDirs Properties dialog box. The Users group is assigned Read & Execute, List Folder Contents, and Read permissions.

16. Clear the Allow Inheritable Permissions From Parent To Propagate To This Object check box.

   A Security message box appears.

17. Read this message box, and then click Remove.

   Notice that the Everyone group no longer has rights to the HomeDirs folder.

   Click the Add button.

   The Select Users, Computers, Or Groups dialog box appears.

18. Verify that Domain*xx*.Contoso.msft appears in the Look In drop-down list.

19. Select the Administrators group.

20. In the Permissions box, select the Allow check box in the Full Control row.

   All check boxes are selected.

21. Click OK.

22. Double-click the HomeDirs folder.

23. Select the John_Smith folder.

24. On the File menu, click Properties.

   The John Smith Properties dialog box appears.

25. Open the Security tab.

    Notice that Administrators and John Smith are granted Full Control permission to this folder. These assignments were automatically granted when you stipulated that the John Smith user account use the \\Srvdc*xx*\HomeDirs\%username% folder as a home folder.

26. Click OK, and then close the HomeDirs window.

27. Log off Student*xx* and log on to Domain*xx* as John_Smith with no password.

28. Double-click the My Computer icon.

    The My Computer window appears.

    Notice that a new network drive icon appears that is pointing to the John_Smith folder on \\Srvdc*xx*\HomeDirs with a Z: drive assignment.

29. Close the My Computer window and log off.

Exercise 4
Changing the Domain Mode

In this exercise, you will use the Active Directory Users And Computers snap-in to change your domain mode. The default operation for Windows 2000 Server is mixed mode. To take advantage of all features relating to groups in Windows 2000 Server, your domain must be in native mode.

▶ **Changing from mixed mode to native mode**

1. Log on to the Contoso domain as Student*xx* with a password of "password."

2. Open the Active Directory Users And Computers snap-in.

3. In the console tree, select the Domain*xx*.Contoso.msft node.

4. On the Action menu, click Properties.

   The Domain*xx*.Contoso.msft Properties dialog box appears.

   Notice that your domain is currently in mixed mode. Also notice the warning about changing the domain mode.

5. Click the Change Mode button.

   An Active Directory message box appears, warning you that this change is irreversible.

6. Click the Yes button.

   The Domain*xx*.Contoso.msft Properties dialog box shows that you changed the domain to native mode.

7. Click OK.

   An Active Directory message box appears, indicating that the operation was successful and telling you that it could take 15 minutes or more for this information to replicate to all domain controllers.

8. Click OK again.

9. Keep the Active Directory Users And Computers snap-in open because you will use it in the next exercise.

Exercise 5
Creating Groups

In this exercise, you will create a global security group. You will then add members to the group. To add members to the group, you add two user accounts, Jane Doe and John Smith, which you created previously. Next you will create a domain local group that you use to assign permissions to gain access to a collection of sales reports. Finally, you provide the members of the global security group with access to the sales reports by adding the global security group to the domain local group.

▶ **Creating a global group, adding members, and organizing user accounts**

1. Log on to the Contoso domain as Student*xx* with a password of "password."
2. Open the Active Directory Users And Computers snap-in.
3. In the console tree, select the Sales node.

   In the Details pane, the Jane Doe user account appears.
4. On the Action menu, point to New, and then click Group.

   The New Object - Group dialog box appears.

   Notice that the Universal radio button in the Global Scope section is available. This option is available only if you are running Active Directory services in native mode.
5. Verify that the Global radio button is selected and that the Security radio button is selected.
6. Type **Sales** in the Group Name text box, and then click OK.

   The group appears in the Details pane of the Sales OU.
7. In the Details pane, double-click Sales.

   The Sales Properties dialog box appears.
8. Open the Members tab.
9. Click the Add button.

   The Select Users, Contacts, Computers, Or Groups dialog box appears, and Domain*xx*.Contoso.msft is shown in the Look In drop-down list.
10. In the list of users and groups, select Jane Doe, press and hold down the CTRL key, and then click John Smith.

    Both user accounts are selected. Notice that Jane Doe is in the Domain*xx*.Contoso.msft/Sales OU and John Smith is in the Domain*xx*.Contoso.msft/Users OU.
11. Click the Add button.

    Jane Doe and John Smith are now members of the Sales global security group.

12. Click OK.

13. Click OK again to close the Sales Properties dialog box.

    For organizational purposes, you have decided to move John Smith to the Sales OU.

14. Select the Users node.

15. Select the John Smith user account in the Details pane.

16. On the Action menu, click Move.

    The Move dialog box appears.

17. Select the Sales node, and then click OK.

    The John Smith user account disappears from the Details pane of the Users OU.

18. In the console tree, select the Sales node.

    John Smith, Jane Doe, and the Sales global security group appear in the Details pane.

19. In the Details pane, double-click the Sales global security group.

    The Sales Properties dialog box appears.

20. Open the Members tab.

    Notice that the John Smith user account remains a member of the group but the Active Directory Folder value is now set to Domain*xx*.Contoso.msft/Sales.

21. Click OK.

22. Leave the Active Directory Users And Computers snap-in open with the Sales node selected.

▶ **Creating and using a domain local group**

In this procedure, you create a domain local group that you use to assign permissions to gain access to sales reports. Because you use the group to assign permissions, you make it a domain local group. You then add members to the group by adding the security global group you created in the previous procedure.

1. Click in the Details pane so that the Sales global security group is no longer selected.

2. On the Action menu, point to New, and then click Group.

    The New Object ‑ Group dialog box appears.

3. In the Group Name text box, type **Reports**.

4. In the Group Scope section, select the Domain Local radio button.

5. In the Group Type section, verify that the Security radio button is selected.

6. Click OK.

    The Reports domain local group appears in the Details pane of the Sales OU.

7. In the Details pane of the Sales OU, double-click Reports.

   The Reports Properties dialog box displays the properties of the group.

8. Open the Members tab.

9. Click the Add button.

   The Select Users, Contacts, Computers, Or Groups dialog box appears.

10. In the Look In drop-down list, select Entire Directory.

    User accounts and groups from all domains and locations appear.

11. At the top of the list, click the Name column.

    The Name column is sorted alphabetically by name (in ascending order).

12. Click the Name column again to sort the list in descending order.

13. Click Sales, click the Add button, and then click OK.

    The Sales group is now a member of the Reports domain local group.

14. Click OK.

15. Close the Active Directory Users And Computers snap-in.

▶ **Implementing NT File System (NTFS) security**

In this procedure, you assign NTFS permissions to the domain local group you created in the last procedure, and then you test access to the Sales organizational unit.

1. Create a folder on the D: drive named Dept.

2. Share the Dept folder as Dept, and in the Comment text box, type **Department share**.

   There is no need to set permissions on the share because the Dept folder is created on an NTFS volume.

3. Click OK.

4. Create a subfolder below the Dept folder, and name it Sales.

5. Select the Sales folder.

6. On the File menu, click Properties.

   The Sales Properties dialog box appears.

7. Open the Security tab.

   Notice that the Everyone system group is granted Full Control permission to this folder.

8. Clear the Allows Inheritable Permissions From Parent To Propagate To This Object check box.

   The Security message box appears.

9. Click the Remove button.

10. Click the Add button.

    The Select Users, Computers, Or Groups dialog box appears.

11. In the Look In drop-down list, select Entire Directory.

12. Select Reports, and then click the Add button.

13. Click OK.

    The Reports domain local group is added and granted Read & Execute, List Folder Contents, and Read permissions.

14. Click the Allow check box in the Write row, and then click OK.

15. Close the Dept window and log off Student*xx*.

16. Log on to Domain*xx* as Jane_Doe with a password of "student," and open the D:\Dept\Sales folder.

17. On the File menu, point to New, and then click Text Document.

    A New Text Document icon appears in the Sales window.

18. Double-click the New Text Document icon.

    Notepad opens and displays the new text document.

19. Type a few letters, and then close Notepad.

    A Notepad message box appears asking if you want to save the changes.

20. Click the Yes button.

21. Close the Sales window.

22. Log off Jane_Doe, and then log on to Domain*xx* as Bob_Train with no password.

    If you are unable to logon as Bob_Train, check to see if you are logging on during a time when you configured Bob Train unable to log on. You configured this in an earlier exercise in this lab.

23. Attempt to open the D:\Dept\Sales folder.

    A Dept message box appears stating that access is denied. Access is not allowed for the Bob Train user account because this account is not a member of the Sales global security group, which was made a member of the Reports domain local group.

24. Click OK to close the Dept window.

25. Log off Bob_Train.

Exercise 6
Creating a Group Policy Object and Setting a Policy

In this exercise, you will create a Group Policy object (GPO) named Domain Policy for your domain. Then you will use the Group Policy snap-in to modify the security settings of the GPO to give domain users the right to log on locally at the domain controllers.

▶ **Creating a GPO at the domain level**

1. Log on to the Contoso domain as Student*xx* with a password of "password."
2. Open the Active Directory Users And Computers snap-in.
3. Open the Domain*xx*.Contoso.msft Properties dialog box.
4. Open the Group Policy tab, and then click the Add button.

    The Add A Group Policy Object Link dialog box appears.
5. Open the All tab.

    Notice that Default Domain Policy is listed. Although you can use this GPO and modify it as you wish, for the purpose of this procedure you will create a new GPO for the domain.
6. Click the middle button of the three buttons on the toolbar.

    A new GPO named New Group Policy Object appears in the list.
7. Name the group policy object Domain Policy, and then click OK.

    The Domain Policy GPO is listed in the Group Policy Object Links column.
8. Click OK.
9. Close the Active Directory Users And Computers snap-in, and log off the computer.

▶ **Modifying security settings**

In this procedure, you use the Group Policy Editor to modify security settings in order to give the Domain Users group the right to log on locally to Srvdc*xx*.

1. Log on to Domain*xx* as Administrator with the password "student."
2. Open the Active Directory Users And Computers snap-in.
3. Select the Domain Controllers node.
4. On the Action menu, click Properties.

    The Domain Controllers Properties dialog box appears.
5. Open the Group Policy tab.
6. In the Group Policy Object Links list, verify that Default Domain Controllers Policy is selected, and then click the Edit button.

7. The Group Policy snap-in appears and displays the Default Domain Controller Policy console tree.

8. In the console tree, expand the Computer Configuration node, and then expand the Windows Settings node.

   The Windows Settings policies appear.

9. Expand the Security Settings node.

   The Security Settings policies appear.

10. Expand the Local Policies node.

    The Local Policies appear.

11. Select the User Rights Assignment node.

    A list of user rights assignment attributes appears in the Details pane.

12. Double-click Log On Locally in the Details pane.

    The Security Policy Setting dialog box appears, displaying details about the Log On Locally policy. Notice that a number of user and group objects are granted this right.

13. Click the Add button.

    The Add User Or Group dialog box appears.

14. Click the Browse button.

    The Select Users Or Groups dialog box appears.

15. In the Name column, select Domain Users, click the Add button, and then click OK.

16. Click OK to close the Add User Or Group dialog box.

    Domain*xx*\Domain Users appears in the list of users and groups with the right to log on locally.

17. Click OK, and then close the Group Policy snap-in.

18. Click OK to close the Domain Controllers Properties dialog box.

    All domain users are now able to log on locally to Srvdc*xx*.

19. Close the Active Directory Users And Computers snap-in and log off the computer.

Exercise 7
Modifying Software Policies

In this exercise, you will create and then modify the Sales OU group policy by removing the Search option and Run option from the Start menu. You will also disable the Lock Workstation policy. You will then view the effects of these software policy modifications. In the last part of this exercise, you will prevent the Sales OU from overriding the group policy of its parent container, the domain.

▶ **Creating and modifying software policies**

1. Log on to the Contoso domain as Studentxx with a password of "password."
2. Open the Active Directory Users And Computers snap-in.
3. Open the Properties dialog box for the Sales OU.
4. Open the Group Policy tab, and then click the Add button.

    The Add A Group Policy Object Link dialog box appears.
5. Open the All tab, and then click the middle button of the three buttons on the toolbar.

    A new GPO appears in the list.
6. Name the new GPO SalesSoftware, and then click OK.
7. With the SalesSoftware GPO selected, click the Edit button.

    The Group Policy snap-in appears.
8. Expand the User Configuration node, and then expand the Administrative Templates node.
9. Select the Start Menu & Task Bar node.

    The policies available for this category appear in the Details pane.
10. In the Details pane, double-click Remove Search Menu From Start Menu.

    The Remove Search Menu From Start Menu Properties dialog box appears.
11. Open the Explain tab to read about this policy.
12. Open the Policy tab, and then select the Enabled radio button.
13. Click OK.
14. Repeat steps 10 through 13 to enable the Remove Run Menu From Start Menu policy.
15. In the console tree, expand the System node, and then select the Logon/Logoff node.

    The policies available for this category appear in the Details pane.
16. In the Details pane, enable the Disable Lock Computer policy.

17. Close the Group Policy snap-in, and then click OK to close the Sales Properties dialog box.

18. Close the Active Directory Users And Computers snap-in.

► **Testing software policies**

In this procedure, you view the effects of the software policies implemented in the previous procedure.

Important Having completed the previous exercises in this lab and the exercises in Lab 6, you should have two user accounts in the Sales OU: Jane Doe and John Smith.

---

1. Log off of Srvdc*xx*.

2. Press CTRL+ALT+DELETE.

    The Log On To Windows dialog box appears. Notice that the Shutdown button is not available. This is controlled by the Shutdown Without Logon policy. Note that Windows 2000 Server does not make this button available by default.

3. Log on to Domain*xx* as Jane_Doe with a password of "student."

4. Click Start.

    Notice that the Search and Run commands do not appear on the Start menu.

5. Log off the computer.

► **Preventing group policy override**

1. Log on to the Contoso domain as Student*xx* with a password of "password."

2. Open the Active Directory Users And Computers snap-in.

3. Open the Properties dialog box for the Sales OU, and then open the Group Policy tab.

4. Verify that SalesSoftware is selected in the Group Policy Objects Links list, and then click the Options button.

    The SalesSoftware Options dialog box appears.

5. Select the No Override: Prevents Other Group Policy Objects From Overriding Policy Set In This One check box, and then click OK.

6. Click OK again, and then close the Active Directory Users And Computers snap-in.

Lab 8: Installing and Configuring Print Sharing and Setting the Printer for Offline Operation

Objectives

After completing this lab, you will be able to

- Add a local printer and configure print sharing.
- Take a printer off line.

Estimated time to complete this lab: 15 minutes

Exercise 1

Installing and Configuring Print Sharing

In this exercise, you will use the Add Printer wizard to add a local printer to your computer and share that printer.

▶ **Adding a local printer and configuring print sharing**

1. Log on to the Contoso domain as Student*xx* with a password of "password."
2. Click Start, point to Settings, and then click Printers.

   The Printers window appears.
3. Double-click the Add Printer icon.

   The Add Printer wizard appears.
4. Click Next.

   The Local Or Network Printer screen appears, and you are prompted for the location of the printer.
5. Select the Local Printer radio button, clear the Automatically Detect And Install My Plug And Play Printer check box, and then click Next.

   The Select The Printer Port screen appears.
6. Select the Create A New Port radio button.

   The Type drop-down list is made active.
7. Click the arrow at the right edge of the Type drop-down list.

   Notice that the available options are Local Port and Standard TCP/IP Port. The port types that are available other than local port depend on the installed network protocols. In this case, TCP/IP is installed, so this protocol-based port is available.
8. Select the Use The Following Port radio button, and then select LPT1 in the list of ports.

   For this exercise, assume that the print device you are adding is directly attached to your computer and using the LPT1 port.
9. Click Next.

   The wizard prompts you for the printer manufacturer and model. You will add an HP LaserJet 5Si printer.

Tip The list of printers is sorted in alphabetical order by manufacturer. If you cannot find a printer name, make sure you are looking in the correct location.

---

10. In the Manufacturers list, select HP, and in the Printers list, select HP LaserJet 5Si.

11. Click Next.

    The Name Your Printer screen appears. In the Printer Name text box, Windows 2000 displays the default printer name, HP LaserJet 5Si. For this exercise, do not change this name.

12. Click Next.

    The Printer Sharing screen appears, prompting you for printer sharing information.

13. Verify that the Share As radio button is selected.

    Notice that you can assign a shared printer name even though you already supplied a printer name. The shared printer name is used to identify a printer on the network and must conform to a specific naming convention. This shared name is different from the printer name you entered previously. The printer name is a description that will appear with the printer's icon in the Printers system folder and in Active Directory services. The share name is kept short for compatibility with other operating systems such as Microsoft Windows 3.x.

14. In the Share As text box, type **Printer1**, and then click Next.

    The Location And Comment screen appears.

Note Windows 2000 displays the values you enter in the Location text box and the Comment text box when a user searches the Active Directory store for a printer. Entering this information is optional, but doing so helps users locate the printer.

---

15. In the Location text box, type **Building 520, Floor 18, Office 1831**. In the Comment text box, type **Black and white output laser printer - high volume**, and then click Next.

    The Print Test Page screen appears.

    Normally, you can print a test page to confirm that your printer is set up properly.

16. Select the No radio button, and then click Next.

    The Completing The Add Printer Wizard screen appears and provides a summary of your installation choices.

17. Confirm the summary of your installation choices, and then click the Finish button.

Windows 2000 copies the necessary printer files, and an icon for the HP LaserJet 5Si printer appears in the Printers window.

Notice that Windows 2000 displays an open hand under the printer icon. This indicates the printer is shared. Also notice the check mark next to the printer, which indicates the printer is the default printer for the print server.

18. Close the Printers window.

▶ **Taking a printer off line and printing a test document**

Taking a printer off line causes documents you send to this printer to be held on the computer while the print device is unavailable. Doing so will prevent error messages about unavailable print devices from occurring in later exercises. Otherwise, Windows 2000 will display such error messages when it attempts to send documents to a print device that is not connected to the computer.

1. If necessary, log on to the Contoso domain as Student*xx* with a password of "password."

2. Open the Printers window, and select the HP LaserJet 5Si icon.

3. On the File menu, click Use Printer Offline.

   Notice that Windows 2000 changes the icon to reflect the fact that the print device is not available. Also notice that the text in the left pane of the Printers window indicates the status of the printer, which in this case is Use Printer Offline.

4. Double-click the HP LaserJet 5Si icon.

   The HP LaserJet 5Si - Use Printer Offline dialog box appears. Notice that the list of documents to be sent to the print device is empty.

5. Click Start, point to Programs, point to Accessories, and then click Notepad.

   The Notepad application appears.

6. Type any sample text that you want.

7. Arrange the Notepad window and the HP LaserJet 5Si - Use Printer Offline dialog box so that you can see the contents of each.

8. On the File menu in Notepad, click Print.

   The Print dialog box appears, allowing you to select the printer and print options.

   The Print dialog box displays the location and comment information you entered when you created the printer, and it shows that the printer is currently off line. You can also use the Find Printer button on the dialog box to search the Active Directory store for a printer.

   Notice that HP LaserJet 5Si is selected as the printer. This printer is automatically selected because HP LaserJet 5Si is the default printer for the print server.

9. Click the Print button.

   Notepad briefly displays a message on your computer stating that the document is printing. On a fast computer, you might not be able to see this message.

   In the HP LaserJet 5Si - Use Printer Offline dialog box, you will see the document waiting to be sent to the print device. The document is held in the print queue because you took the printer off line. If the printer were on line, the document would be sent to the print device.

10. Close Notepad, and click the No button when prompted to save changes to your document.

11. On the Printer menu in the HP LaserJet 5Si - Use Printer Offline dialog box, click Cancel All Documents.

    A Printers message box appears asking if you are sure you want to cancel all documents for HP LaserJet 5Si.

12. Click the Yes button.

    The document is removed.

13. Close the HP LaserJet 5Si - Use Printer Offline dialog box.

14. Close the Printers window.

Lab 9: Configuring Network Protocols and Services

Objectives

After completing this lab, you will be able to

- Configure and test TCP/IP.
- Install and configure Dynamic Host Configuration Protocol (DHCP).
- Install and configure Windows Internet Name Service (WINS).
- Configure DNS.

Estimated time to complete this lab: 60 minutes

Exercise 1
Configuring and Testing TCP/IP

In this exercise, you will use two TCP/IP utilities, ipconfig and ping, to verify the TCP/IP configuration of Srvdc*xx*.

▶ **Verifying a computer's TCP/IP configuration**

1. Log on to the Contoso domain as Student*xx* with a password of "password."

2. Open a command prompt window.

3. At the command prompt, type **ipconfig /all | more**, and then press ENTER. (The vertical line between the words "all" and "more" is the dashed line typically located on the backslash [\] key.)

   The Windows 2000 IP Configuration utility displays the TCP/IP configuration of the network adapter or adapters configured on your computer.

4. Press the Spacebar as necessary to display any results that you cannot see. Use the information displayed to complete as much of the following table as possible. Some values entered in the table were set through configuration procedures in earlier exercises.

Setting	Value
Host Name	Srvdc*xx*
Primary DNS Suffix	Domain*xx*.Contoso.msft
Description	_____
Physical Address	_____
Subnet Mask	_____
DHCP Enabled	_____
IP Address	_____
Default Gateway	_____
DNS Servers	_____

5. Press the Spacebar as necessary to return to the command prompt.

6. Type **ping 127.0.0.1**, and then press ENTER.

   This IP address is called the *loop-back address* and is used to verify that the TCP/IP stack is functioning properly.

A response similar to the following indicates a successful ping:

```
Pinging 127.0.0.1 with 32 bytes of data:
Reply from 127.0.0.1: bytes=32 time<10ms TTL=128
Reply from 127.0.0.1: bytes=32 time<10ms TTL=128
Reply from 127.0.0.1: bytes=32 time<10ms TTL=128
Reply from 127.0.0.1: bytes=32 time<10ms TTL=128

Ping statistics for 127.0.0.1:
Packets: Sent = 4, Received = 4, Lost = 0 <0% loss>,

Approximate round trip times in milliseconds:
Minimum = 0ms, Maximum = 0ms, Average = 0ms
```

7. Close the command prompt window.

Exercise 2
Installing and Configuring DHCP

In this exercise, you will install and configure the DHCP service. You will create a scope and configure a small range of addresses for the scope.

▶ **Installing the DHCP service**

1. Click Start, point to Programs, and then point to Administrative Tools.

   Notice that DHCP appears in the list of administrative tools. This is only the DHCP snap-in; DHCP is not yet installed on the server.

2. Open the Add/Remove Programs utility in Control Panel.

3. Click the Add/Remove Windows Components button in the left frame.

   The Windows Components wizard appears.

4. In the Components list, select Networking Services, but do not click or change the status of the check box to the left of this option.

Note The Networking Services check box is already selected because some networking services have already been installed on Srvdc*xx*.

5. Click the Details button.

   The Networking Services dialog box appears.

   In the Subcomponents Of Networking Services list, select the Dynamic Host Configuration Protocol (DHCP) check box.

6. Click OK.

7. Click Next.

   The Configuring Components screen appears as the configuration changes are being made. A Copying Files message box appears as DHCP files are copied into the operating system folders.

   After the files are copied, the Completing The Windows Components Wizard screen appears.

8. Click the Finish button.

9. Close the Add/Remove Programs window.

10. Close the Control Panel window.

▶ **Creating and configuring a DHCP scope**

1. Open the DHCP snap-in.

2. In the console tree, double-click the Srvdc*xx*.Domain*xx*.Contoso.msft [10.1.10.*xx*] node.

   A message about configuring DHCP appears in the Details pane.

3. Read the message appearing in the Details pane.

4. On the Action menu, click New Scope.

   The New Scope wizard appears.

5. Click Next.

   The Scope Name screen appears.

6. In the Name text box, type **Srvdcxx Scope**.

7. In the Description text box, type **Training network**, and then click Next.

   The IP Address Range screen appears.

8. In the Start IP Address text box, type **10.1.1xx.70**, where *xx* is the two-digit number from your computer name and user ID.

9. In the End IP Address text box, type **10.1.1xx.90**.

   Notice that the subnet mask is set to a standard class A mask, 255.0.0.0. All bits in the first octet are set to 1.

10. Click Next.

    The Add Exclusions screen appears.

11. In the Start IP Address box, type **10.1.1xx.76**.

12. In the End IP Address text box, type **10.1.1xx.80**.

13. Click the Add button.

    Notice that 10.1.1xx.76 to 10.1.1xx.80 appears in the Excluded Addresses Range text box.

14. Click Next.

    The Lease Duration screen appears. Read the information on this page, and notice that the default lease duration is eight days.

15. Click Next to accept the default lease duration.

    The Configure DHCP Options screen appears, asking if you would like to configure the most common DHCP options now.

16. Select the No, I Will Configure These Options Later radio button, and then click Next.

    The Completing The New Scope Wizard screen appears.

17. Read the instructions on this screen, and then click the Finish button.

    The new scope appears in the console tree of the DHCP snap-in.

    The red arrow pointing down indicates that the scope is not activated. You will activate the scope in the next procedure.

▶ **Adding a reservation to a DHCP scope and activating the scope**

1. In the console tree of the DHCP snap-in, expand the Scope [10.0.0.0] Srvdc*xx* Scope node.

2. Select the Reservations node, and read the message appearing in the Details pane.

3. On the Action menu, click New Reservation.

   The New Reservation dialog box appears.

4. In the Reservation Name text box, type **Srvdcxx**.

5. In the IP Address text box, notice the first octet is entered for you. In the last three octets, type **1.1xx.76**. The entire box should read 10.1.1xx.76.

6. In the MAC Address text box, type **005004b43a23**.

7. In the Description text box, type **Reservation made by** *your name*.

   Notice that DHCP, BOOTP, or both types of clients can be configured to use this reservation. A BOOTP client could be a device such as a legacy terminal or router. The option that you select will determine the types of client requests that are answered by the DHCP server. Dynamic BOOTP scopes are also supported. For more information on these configuration options, see the section in the DHCP online help file titled "Supporting BOOTP Clients." This help file is available in the MSDN library.

8. In the Supported Types group, select the DHCP Only radio button, and then click the Add button.

   Another New Reservation dialog box appears.

9. Click the Close button.

   Notice that the reservation appears in the Details pane.

10. In the console tree, select the Scope [10.0.0.0] Srvdcxx Scope node.

11. On the Action menu, click Activate.

    Notice that the red down arrow to the left of the scope's name disappears. Notice also that the down arrow for Srvdcxx.Domainxx.Contoso.msft [10.1.10.1] remains.

    At this point, the DHCP server will have to be authorized. Someone in the Enterprise Administration group (in this case, your instructor) must do this. The process could take several minutes.

12. To check if the server has been authorized, press the F5 key to refresh the display.

    When a green up arrow appears next to Srvdcxx.Domainxx.Contoso.msft [10.1.10.1], the DHCP Service has been authorized.

▶   **Configuring scope options**

In this procedure, you configure DHCP so that the preferred DNS servers and DNS domain name are sent to the DHCP client upon registration. This procedure is similar to setting server options, which apply to all DHCP clients using this server, and setting individual client options.

1. Open the DHCP snap-in.

2. In the console tree, expand the Srvdc*xx*.Domain*xx*.Contoso.msft [10.1.10.1] node, expand the Scope [10.0.0.0] Srvdc*xx* Scope node, and then select the Scope Options node.

3. On the Action menu, click Configure Options.

   The Scope Options dialog box appears.

4. Select the 006 DNS Servers check box.

   Controls in the Data Entry group are activated.

5. In the Server Name text box, type **Srvdc*xx***, and then click the Resolve button.

   The IP address for your computer appears in the IP Address text box.

6. Click the Add button.

7. In the Available Options list, select the 015 DNS Domain Name check box.

8. In the String Value text box, type **domain*xx*.contoso.msft**, and then click OK.

   DNS data will now be downloaded to DHCP client computers within this scope.

9. Close the DHCP snap-in.

Exercise 3
Installing and Configuring WINS

In this exercise, you will install WINS on Srvdcxx. After the installation, you will configure additional settings for the DHCP service so that it can provide support for WINS.

Note WINS is required only for legacy support. In your small training network and in a homogeneous network of Windows 2000 clients and servers, WINS is not necessary because all computers running Windows 2000 use DNS for name resolution. This exercise is intended to teach you how to perform a basic installation and configuration of WINS.

▶ **Installing WINS**

1. Log on to the Contoso domain as Studentxx with a password of "password."
2. In Control Panel, open the Add/Remove Programs utility.
3. In the left frame, click the Add/Remove Windows Components button.

   The Windows Components wizard appears.
4. In the Components list, select Networking Services, but do not click or change the status of the check box to the left of this option.
5. Click the Details button.

   The Networking Services dialog box appears.

   In the Subcomponents Of Networking Services list, select the Windows Internet Name Service (WINS) check box.
6. Click OK.
7. Click Next.

   The Configuring Components screen appears.
8. If the Files Needed dialog box appears, ensure that the path name in the Copy Files From drop-down list is \\Instructor01\WinDist, and then click OK.

   The Completing The Windows Components Wizard screen appears.
9. Click the Finish button.
10. Close the Add/Remove Programs window.
11. Close the Control Panel window.

▶ **Configuring DHCP to support WINS**

In this procedure, you configure WINS settings in the DHCP snap-in. To get practice setting server options, you will use the Server Options node. You can also configure these settings by using Scope Options if you want them to apply only to a specific scope or even to a specific DHCP client.

1. Open the DHCP snap-in.
2. In the console tree, select the Server Options node.
3. On the Action menu, click Configure Options.

   The Server Options dialog box appears.
4. In the Available Options list, select the 044 WINS/NBNS Servers check box.
5. In the Server Name text box, type **Srvdcxx**, and then click the Resolve button.

   Your server's IP address appears in the IP Address text box.
6. Click the Add button.
7. In the Available Options list, select the 046 WINS/NBT Node Type check box.
8. In the Byte text box, change the text box entry to **0x8**.

   0x8 sets the node type to h-node. Node type determines how WINS resolution occurs at a client computer. H-node instructs the client to check with the WINS server first (p-node point-to-point communication with the name server) and then send out a b-node broadcast if necessary.
9. Click the OK button.

   The two server options appear in the Details pane.
10. Close the DHCP snap-in.

Exercise 4
Configuring DNS

In this exercise, you will delete and re-create a forward lookup zone, create a reverse lookup zone, configure Dynamic DNS, and test your DNS server.

▶   **Configuring a forward lookup zone and a reverse lookup zone**

1. Log on to the Contoso domain as Student*xx* with a password of "password."

2. Click Start, point to Programs, point to Administrative Tools, and then click DNS.

    The DNS snap-in appears.

3. In the console tree, expand the Srvdc*xx* node, and then select the Forward Lookup Zones node.

4. On the Action menu, click New Zone.

    The New Zone wizard appears.

5. Click Next.

    The Zone Type screen appears.

6. Verify that the Standard Primary radio button is selected, and then click Next.

    The Zone Name screen appears.

7. Type **domain*xx*.contoso.msft**, and then click Next.

    The Zone File screen appears.

8. Verify that the Create A New File With This File Name radio button is selected and that the name of the file to be created is Domain*xx*.Contoso.msft.dns.

9. Click Next.

    The Completing The New Zone Wizard screen appears.

10. Review the information on this screen, and then click the Finish button.

    The Domain*xx*.Contoso.msft node is added to the console tree.

11. Select the Domain*xx*.Contoso.msft node.

    Notice that Start of Authority, Name Server, and Host records are generated. Srvdc*xx* is now able to resolve host names to IP addresses by using the lookup zone file.

12. In the console tree, select the Reverse Lookup Zones node.

13. On the Action menu, click New Zone.

    The New Zone wizard appears.

14. Click Next.

    The Zone Type screen appears.

15. Verify that the Standard Primary radio button is selected, and then click Next.

    The Reverse Lookup Zone screen appears.

16. Verify that the Network ID radio button is selected.

17. In the Network ID text box, type **10.1.10**.

    The Reverse Lookup Zone Name text box at the bottom of the screen now contains 10.1.10.in-addr.arpa.

18. Click Next.

    The Zone File screen appears.

19. Verify that the Create A New File With This File Name radio button is selected and that the name of the file to be created is 10.1.10.in-addr.arpa.dns.

20. Click Next.

    The Completing The New Zone Wizard screen appears.

21. Review the information on the screen, and then click the Finish button.

    The 10.1.10.x Subnet node is added to the console tree.

Note After creating a DNS zone, it is common to add the DNS configuration information to the DHCP service. You completed this procedure in the DHCP exercise earlier in this lab.

▶ **Configuring Dynamic DNS**

1. In the console tree, select the Domain*xx*.Contoso.msft node, which is located under the Forward Lookup Zones node.

2. On the Action menu, click Properties.

    The Domain*xx*.Contoso.msft Properties dialog box appears.

3. In the Allow Dynamic Updates drop-down list, select Yes, and then click OK.

    Dynamic DNS is now configured for the forward lookup zone.

4. In the console tree, select the 10.1.10.x Subnet node.

5. On the Action menu, click Properties.

    The 10.1.10.x Subnet Properties dialog box appears.

6. In the Allow Dynamic Updates drop-down list, select Yes, and then click OK.

    Dynamic DNS is now configured for the reverse lookup zone.

▶ **Testing and configuring DNS**

In this procedure, you confirm that the DNS service is working properly and further configure DNS using the DNS snap-in.

1. In the console tree, select the Srvdc*xx* node.

2. On the Action menu, click Properties.

    The Srvdc*xx* Properties dialog box appears.

3. Open the Monitoring tab.

4. Under Select A Test Type, select the A Simple Query Against This DNS Server check box and the A Recursive Query To Other DNS Servers check box.

5. Click the Test Now button.

   In the Test Results box, you will see PASS in the Simple Query column and FAIL in the Recursive Query column.

6. Click OK.

7. In the console tree, select the 10.1.10.x Subnet node.

   Notice that this reverse lookup zone shows two records in the Details pane: Start of Authority and Name Server.

8. On the Action menu, click New Pointer.

   The New Resource Record dialog box appears.

9. In the last octet of the Host IP Number text box, type *xx*, where *xx* is the two-digit number included in your computer name and your student logon name.

10. In the Host Name text box, type **srvdc*xx*.domain*xx*.contoso.msft.** (Make sure to include the period after msft.)

11. Click OK.

    A pointer record appears in the Details pane.

12. Close the DNS snap-in.

13. Open a command prompt window, type **nslookup**, and then press ENTER.

    The default server is listed as Srvdc*xx*.Domain*xx*.Contoso.msft, and the address is listed as 10.1.10.*xx*.

14. Type **ls domain*xx*.contoso.msft**, and then press ENTER.

    Notice that the NS (name server) and A (host) records are displayed as a result of this DNS query.

15. Type **exit**, and then press ENTER.

    Close the command prompt window.

Lab 10: Configuring Routing and Remote Access Services (RRAS)

Objectives

After completing this lab, you will be able to

- Enable RRAS and examine a basic configuration.
- Configure a RAS connection.

Estimated time to complete this lab: 25 minutes

Exercise 1
Enabling RRAS and Examining a Basic Configuration

RRAS is, by default, in a disabled state on your server. In this exercise, you will enable RRAS and then examine its default configuration.

▶   **Enabling RRAS**

1. Log on to the Contoso domain as Student*xx* with a password of "password."

2. Click Start, point to Programs, point to Administrative Tools, and then click Routing And Remote Access.

   The Routing And Remote Access snap-in appears.

3. Select the Srvdc*xx* (local) node and read the message that appears in the Details pane.

4. On the Action menu, click Configure And Enable Routing And Remote Access.

   The Routing And Remote Access Server Setup wizard appears.

5. Click Next.

   The Common Configurations screen appears. Notice that there are five paths that you can follow in configuring an RRAS server. In the next step, you will examine these various options before configuring the RRAS server to act as a RAS server.

6. Verify that the Internet Connection Server radio button is selected, and then click Next.

   The Internet Connection Server Setup screen appears. Notice that the RRAS server is configured in one of two ways in order to provide all computers on the network with access to the Internet. If you select the Set Up Internet Connection Sharing (ICS) radio button and click Next, you are provided online instructions on how to connect a single office. If you select the Set Up A Router With The Network Address Translation (NAT) Routing Protocol radio button and click Next, the Routing And Remote Access Server Setup wizard continues to step you through the configuration process. NAT allows you to configure the server to send and receive packets from the Internet on behalf of other client computers on the intranet. Only the hardware on the RRAS server that connects to the Internet requires an IP address that is valid and legal on the Internet.

7. Click the Back button to return to the Common Configurations screen.

   Read the following instructions but do not complete them:

   a. Select the Remote Access Server radio button to configure the RRAS server for RAS dial-in access.

   b. Select the Virtual Private Network (VPN) Server radio button to configure the server for Point-to-Point Tunneling Protocol (PPTP) and Layer 2 Tunneling Protocol (L2TP) access. VPN allows remote access clients to connect to a public network such as the Internet and then establish a secure remote access connection to the RRAS server.

  c. Select the Network Router radio button to configure the RRAS server so that packets can be transmitted between networks.

  d. Select the Manually Configured Server radio button to use the Routing And Remote Access snap-in to configure the RRAS server.

Note An RRAS server can be configured to perform a combination of the functions appearing on the Common Configurations screen. The purpose of this screen is to help you get started with RRAS. Further configuration is completed by using the Routing And Remote Access snap-in or the Net Shell (netsh) utility.

8. Select the Manually Configured Server radio button, and then click Next.

   The Completing The Routing And Remote Access Server Setup Wizard screen appears.

9. Click the Finish button.

   A Routing And Remote Access message box appears, stating that the Routing And Remote Access service has been installed. You are asked whether the service should be started.

10. Click the Yes button.

   The Starting Routing And Remote Access message box and the Completing Initialization message box appear as the service is being started. When the process is complete, the Srvcd*xx* (local) node is marked with a green arrow rather than a red one, indicating that RRAS is configured and enabled on the computer.

▶ **Examining a default RRAS configuration**

The purpose of this procedure is to introduce you to the features appearing in the Routing And Remote Access snap-in. You will examine the default remote access and router settings.

Caution Do not change any settings while examining the default configuration.

1. In the console tree, expand the Srvdc*xx* (local) node.
2. Click the Action menu.

   Notice that the Disable Routing And Remote Access command is now available because the RRAS server is enabled and configured.

3. On the Action menu, click Properties.

   The Srvdc*xx* (local) Properties dialog box appears.

   Notice that the default settings appearing on the General tab show that the server has been configured as a LAN router, a demand-dial routing router, and a remote access server.

4. Open the Security tab.

   Notice that the authentication provider and the accounting provider are both Microsoft Windows.

5. Click the Authentication Methods button.

   The Authentication Methods dialog box appears. Notice that MS-CHAP and MS-CHAP version 2 are selected. To troubleshoot authentication problems, you can select the Allow Remote Systems To Connect Without Authentication check box. You can also select other authentication methods based on the needs of the dial-up client and your security requirements.

6. Click the Cancel button, and then open the IP tab.

   Notice that the Enable IP Routing check box and the Allow IP-Based Remote Access And Demand-Dial Connections check box are selected. IP routing allows dial-up clients to access the entire network. If you want dial-up clients to access resources on the RRAS server only, clear the Enable IP Routing check box. The Allow IP-Based Remote Access And Demand-Dial Connections option allows RRAS to use Internet Protocol Control Protocol (IPCP) to negotiate the use of IP over the remote access or demand-dial interface. Notice also that the IP tab is used to specify either IP address allocation via DHCP or a static pool configured on the RRAS server.

7. Open the PPP tab.

   From this tab, you can configure global Point-to-Point Protocol (PPP) support settings for remote access clients.

8. Open the Event Logging tab.

   From here, you can configure the amount of information you want to collect about RRAS events occurring on the server. For troubleshooting, you can select the Log The Maximum Amount Of Information radio button and the Enable Point-To-Point Protocol (PPP) Logging check box. To optimize the server's performance, select the Disable Event Logging radio button.

9. Click the Cancel button.

10. In the console tree, select the Routing Interfaces node.

    The list of router interfaces appears in the Details pane. Loopback is the local protocol stack on the RRAS server. Local Area Connection is the RRAS server's network interface card that is connected to your network. Internal is the routing function in RRAS. If routing is disabled, then Internal has a status of non-operational.

11. In the console tree, select the Ports node.

    Notice that your modem or WAN device is listed in the Details pane. The Parallel device appearing in the Details pane is available to support direct cable connections between two computers. If you have a single LPT port designated as LPT1, then the name of this connection is Direct Parallel (LPT1). If a remote client has connected to a port but performance is poor or you are troubleshooting the connection, select the port to which the client is connected, and on the Action menu, click Status. This will show you network registration, statistics, and error information about the connection.

12. On the Action menu, click Properties.

The Ports Properties dialog box appears. From this dialog box, you configure the number of ports allowed for each port type (only applicable to VPN connections) and whether connections on this port type are inbound only or inbound and outbound. You can also configure the phone number for the device. This feature is used if the Called-Station-ID is configured for remote access policy, the dial-up hardware and driver software do not support caller ID, or you use multi-link with the bandwidth allocation protocol (BAP) enabled. If you are configuring a VPN port, enter the IP address of the port rather than a phone number.

13. Click the Cancel button.

14. In the console tree, select the Remote Access Clients node.

If a remote client is connected to the RRAS server, the Details pane shows the connected user, call duration, and number of ports allocated to the call (multilink).

15. In the console tree, expand the IP Routing node, and then select the General node.

Notice that the information appearing in the Details pane looks similar to the information appearing in the Details pane of Routing Interfaces.

16. On the Action menu, click New Routing Protocol.

The New Routing Protocol dialog box appears.

Notice that there are three protocols appearing by default: NAT, OSPF, and RIP version 2.

17. Click the Cancel button.

18. In the Details pane, select Internal, and then click the Action menu.

Notice that many commands for monitoring the interface are available on the Action menu. The Properties command is used to configure general router settings in the RRAS server.

Examine the properties of the Internal interface and the Local Area Connection interface, and then return to the Routing And Remote Access snap-in console.

The Static Routes node in the console tree is used to view and configure additional routes to other networks. This tool is the graphical equivalent of the Route command line utility.

The DHCP Relay Agent node allows DHCP request and response messages to be sent from one network to another. This feature allows a single server running the DHCP service to provide IP address configuration information to

DHCP (modified BOOTP) and BOOTP-enabled clients on other networks accessible by the router.

The IGMP node allows for the configuration of Internet Group Messaging Protocol.

19. In the console tree, select the Remote Access Logging node.

Note If you are using a RADIUS server for authentication and logging, the Remote Access Logging folder does not appear in RRAS.

Local File appears in the Details pane, and the description column shows the path to the LogFiles folder.

20. In the Details pane, double-click Local File.

The Local File Properties dialog box appears.

The Settings tab and the Local File tab are used to configure logging. Use the Settings tab to configure the amount of information you want to log about remote access authentication, administration, and status.

21. Open the Local File tab.

Use the Local File tab to configure the log file format, when new logs are generated, and where the logs are stored. Moving the log file directory (folder) to another partition other than the boot partition is advisable.

22. Click the Cancel button.

23. In the console tree, select the Remote Access Policies node.

The default remote access policy, Allow Access If Dial-In Permission Is Enabled, appears in the Details pane.

24. Double-click Allow Access If Dial-In Permission Is Enabled.

The Allow Access If Dial-In Permission Is Enabled Properties dialog box appears.

25. Click the Edit button.

The Time Of Day Constraints dialog box appears.

Notice that dial-in is allowed around the clock.

26. Click the Cancel button.

Notice that the Deny Remote Access Permission radio button is selected. This means that unless this profile is overridden on a per-user basis, users who depend on access based on a profile will always be denied access.

27. Click the Add button.

The Select Attribute dialog box appears. This dialog box lists the various connection attributes that can be associated with this profile. Users who meet the conditions specified in the profile are either allowed or denied access.

28. Click the Cancel button.

29. Click the Edit Profile button.

    The Edit Dial-In Profile dialog box appears.

30. Explore the various tabs and settings available for editing the profile. Notice that many of the settings configured for the profile can also be set separately from the profile in the Routing And Remote Access snap-in.

31. Click the Cancel button.

32. Click the Cancel button to close the Allow Access If Dial-In Permission Is Enabled Properties dialog box.

33. Close the Routing And Remote Access snap-in.

Note RRAS can also be configured from the command prompt by using the netsh utility (Net Shell) rather than using the Routing And Remote Access snap-in.

Exercise 2
Configuring and Monitoring a RAS Connection

In this exercise, you will configure dial-in access and set up accounting and logging.

▶ **Allowing and denying dial-in access to user accounts**

1. Open the Active Directory Users And Computers snap-in.

2. In the console tree, select the Sales node.

   The objects in the Sales OU appear in the Details pane.

3. In the Details pane, double-click Jane Doe.

   The Jane Doe Properties dialog box appears.

4. Open the Dial-In tab.

5. Select the Allow Access radio button, and then click OK.

6. In the Details pane of the Active Directory Users And Computers snap-in, open the Properties dialog box for John Smith, and then open the Dial-In tab.

7. Verify that the Control Access Through Remote Access Policy radio button is selected, and then click OK.

8. In the console tree, select the Users node.

   The objects in the Users container appear in the Details pane.

9. Access the dial-in properties for Bob Train.

10. Select the Deny Access radio button, and then click OK.

11. Close the Active Directory Users And Computers snap-in.

▶ **Configuring the RRAS server for Windows account logging and event logging**

1. Open the Routing And Remote Access snap-in.

2. In the console tree, select the Remote Access Logging node.

3. In the Details pane, double-click Local File.

   The Local File Properties dialog box appears.

4. Select the Log Authentication Requests check box.

5. Click OK.

6. In the console tree, select the Srvdc*xx* (local) node.

7. On the Action menu, click Properties.

   The Srvdc*xx* (local) Properties dialog box appears.

8. Open the Event Logging tab.

9. Select the Log The Maximum Amount Of Information radio button, and select the Enable Point-To-Point Protocol (PPP) Logging check box.

10. Click OK.

    A Routing And Remote Access message box appears asking whether you want to restart the router.

11. Click the Yes button.

    A number of message boxes appear as Routing And Remote Access is stopped and restarted.

12. After Routing And Remote Access has been stopped and restarted, close the Routing And Remote Access snap-in.

Lab 11: Installing, Configuring, and Analyzing Security

Objectives

After completing this lab, you will be able to

- Install and configure Microsoft Certificate Services.
- Configure the certification authority (CA).
- Configure and use file encryption.
- Create and use the Security Analysis And Configuration snap-in.

Estimated time to complete this lab: 35 minutes

Exercise 1
Installing and Configuring Certificate Services

In this exercise, you will install an enterprise subordinate CA and use this CA to issue, install, and revoke certificates. An enterprise root CA has been created on the Instructor01 server, and your CA will be a subordinate to that.

▶ **Installing Certificate Services and configuring the certification authority**

In this procedure, you install Certificate Services on Srvdc*xx*, which will act as an enterprise subordinate CA.

1. Log on to the Contoso domain as Student*xx* with a password of "password."
2. Open the Add/Remove Programs utility in Control Panel.
3. In the left pane, click the Add/Remove Windows Components button.

    The Windows Components wizard appears.
4. Select the Certificate Services check box.

    A Microsoft Certificate Services message box appears, stating that once Certificate Services is installed, the computer cannot be renamed and it cannot join or be removed from a domain.
5. Click the Yes button.
6. On the Windows Components screen, click the Details button.

    The Certificate Services dialog box appears.

    Notice that Certificate Services subcomponents include both the service used to create a certification authority and a Web enrollment form for submitting requests and retrieving certificates from the computer running as a certification authority.
7. Click OK.
8. Click Next.

    The Certification Authority Type screen appears.
9. Select each available radio button, and read the text appearing in the Description box.

    Notice that the stand-alone options run independently from Active Directory services. Thus, they can be used in the presence or absence of Active Directory services. If Active Directory services is present, the stand-alone CA types will use it. Subordinate CA types are dependent on the presence of a CA higher up in the CA hierarchy.
10. Verify that the Enterprise Subordinate CA radio button is selected, and select the Advanced Options check box.
11. Click Next.

    The Public And Private Key Pair screen appears.

Notice that there are a number of Cryptographic Service Providers (CSPs), each having one or more associated hash algorithms used to generate key pairs. From this screen you can also view certificates, specify the key length, or import keys.

12. Verify that the Microsoft Base Cryptographic Provider v1.0 CSP is selected and that the SHA-1 hash algorithm is selected, and then click Next.

   The CA Identifying Information screen appears.

13. Type the information from the following table into the text boxes on the screen.

Text box	Value to type
CA Name	Domainxx CA
Organization	Contoso Corporation
Organizational Unit	Contoso Press
City	Seattle
State Or Province	Washington
E-mail	ca-test@contoso.com
CA Description	Subordinate CA for training only

   Notice that the parent CA determines the length of time this certificate is valid.

14. Click Next.

   The Data Storage Location screen appears.

   Notice that the certificate database and the log file are stored in the CertLog folder, which is stored on the boot partition. If disk capacity on the boot partition is limited, consider specifying another secure partition for the certificate database and log file.

15. Click Next.

   The CA Certificate Request screen appears.

16. Verify that the Send The Request Directly To A CA Already On The Network radio button is selected, and then click the Browse button.

   The Select Certification Authority dialog box appears.

17. In the Select A Certification Authority To Send The Request list, select Enterprise CA, and then click OK.

Note If the Select Certification Authority dialog box doesn't appear, type **Instructor01** in the Computer Name text box, and then select Enterprise CA in the Parent CA drop-down list.

The Computer Name text box now points to Instructor01.Contoso.msft, and Enterprise CA appears in the Parent CA drop-down list.

18. Click Next.

A Microsoft Certificate Services message box appears, stating that Internet Information Services is running on the computer and warning you that it must be stopped in order to continue.

19. Click OK.

The Configuring Components screen appears as software is installed and configured.

20. If the Files Needed dialog box appears, verify that \\Instructor01\\Windist appears in the Copy Files From drop-down list, and then click OK.

After the components are installed, the Completing The Windows Components Wizard screen appears.

21. Click the Finish button.

22. Close the Add/Remove Programs window.

23. Close the Control Panel window.

▶ **Running Certificate Services**

In this procedure, you generate, install, and revoke a certificate. You will use the Certificate Enrollment URL and the Certification Authority snap-in to complete this procedure.

1. Open the Certification Authority snap-in from the Administrative Tools program group.

2. In the console tree, expand the Domain*xx* CA node.

3. Select the Pending Requests node.

4. Click Start, and then click Run.

The Run dialog box appears.

5. In the Open text box, type **http://srvdc*xx*/certsrv**, and then click OK.

The Internet Connection wizard appears.

6. Select the I Want To Set Up My Internet Connection Manually, Or I Want To Connect Through A Local Area Network (LAN) radio button.

7. Click Next.

The Setting Up Your Internet Connection screen appears.

8. Select the I Connect Through A Local Area Network (LAN) radio button.

9. Click Next.

The Local Area Network Internet Configuration screen appears.

10. Clear the Automatic Discovery Of Proxy Server check box.

11. Click Next.

The Set Up Your Internet Mail Account screen appears.

12. Select the No radio button, and then click Next.

    The Completing The Internet Connection Wizard screen appears.

13. Click the Finish button.

    Microsoft Internet Explorer displays the Certificate Services Welcome page.

14. Read the information on this page, and then verify that the Request A Certificate radio button is selected.

15. Click Next.

    The Choose Request Type page appears, and the User Certificate Request radio button is selected.

16. Click Next.

    The User Certificate - Identifying Information page appears.

17. Click the More Options button.

    Notice that the CSP selected is the CSP type you specified during installation of Certificate Services.

18. Click the Submit button.

    The Certificate Issued page appears.

19. Minimize Internet Explorer and restore the Certification Authority snap-in.

20. Select the Issued Certificates node.

    Your certificate request is listed in the Details pane. If you don't see the certificate, press F5 to refresh the screen.

21. Double-click the certificate appearing in the Details pane.

    The Certificate dialog box appears.

22. Open the Details tab, and then select Issuer.

    Notice that the information appearing in the bottom box is the information you typed into the CA Identifying Information screen.

23. Click OK.

24. Minimize the Certification Authority snap-in, and then restore Internet Explorer.

25. Click the Install This Certificate hyperlink.

    The Certificate Installed page appears, stating that you have successfully installed a certificate.

26. Close Internet Explorer.

27. Restore the Certification Authority snap-in, and then select the certificate in the Details pane.

28. On the Action menu, point to All Tasks, and then click Revoke Certificate.

    The Certificate Revocation dialog box appears.

29. In the Reason Code drop-down list, select Key Compromise, and then click the Yes button.

    The certificate is removed from the Details pane.

30. In the console tree, select the Revoked Certificates node.

    The revoked certificate appears in the Details pane.

31. On the Action menu, point to All Tasks, and then click Publish.

    The Certificate Revocation List dialog box appears, stating that the previous list is still valid.

32. Click the Yes button.

33. Close the Certification Authority snap-in.

34. Open Internet Explorer, and go to *http://srvdcxx/certsrv*.

    The Certificate Services Welcome page appears.

35. Select the Retrieve The CA Certificate Or Certificate Revocation List radio button, and then click Next.

    The Retrieve The CA Certificate Or Certificate Revocation List page appears.

36. Click the Download Latest Certificate Revocation List hyperlink.

    The File Download dialog box appears.

37. Select the Open This File From Its Current Location radio button, and then click OK.

    The Certificate Revocation List dialog box appears.

38. Open the Revocation List tab.

39. In the Revoked Certificates list, select the revoked certificate, which appears as a serial number.

    In the Revocation Entry list, the serial number of the revoked certificate, the date of revocation, and the reason for revocation appear.

40. Click OK.

41. Close Internet Explorer.

Exercise 2
Configuring and Using File Encryption

In this exercise, you will configure a data recovery policy in the domain and then encrypt a folder.

▶ **Configuring a data recovery policy for the domain**

Recovery policy is configured by default when the first domain controller is installed. As a result, a self-signed certificate assigns the domain administrator as the recovery agent. In this procedure, you will manually add Student*xx* as the recovery agent before using Encrypting File System (EFS).

1. Log on to the Contoso domain as Student*xx* with a password of "password."
2. Open the Active Directory Users And Computers snap-in from the Administrative Tools group.
3. Select the Domain*xx*.Contoso.msft node.
4. On the Action menu, click Properties.

   The Domain*xx*.Contoso.msft Properties dialog box appears.
5. Open the Group Policy tab, and then select Domain Policy in the list of group policy objects.
6. Click the Edit button.

   The Group Policy snap-in appears.
7. Under the Computer Configuration node, expand the Windows Settings node.
8. Expand the Security Settings node.
9. Expand the Public Key Policies node.
10. Select the Encrypted Data Recovery Agents node.
11. On the Action menu, click Create.

    The Certificate Request wizard appears.
12. Click Next.

    The Certificate Template screen appears.
13. Verify that EFS Recovery Agent is selected, and then click Next.

    The Certificate Friendly Name And Description screen appears.
14. In the Friendly Name text box, type **Student*xx* EFS certificate**, and then click Next.

    The Completing The Certificate Request Wizard screen appears.
15. Review the information on the screen, and then click the Finish button.

    A Certificate Request Wizard message box appears.

16. Click the Install Certificate button.

    Another Certificate Request Wizard message box appears, stating that the certificate was installed successfully.

17. Click OK.

    Student*xx* is added to the Details pane.

18. Select the Student *xx* entry in the Details pane.

19. On the Action menu, click Properties.

    The Student *xx* Properties dialog box appears.

20. View the properties, and then click OK.

21. Close the Group Policy snap-in.

22. Click OK to close the Domain*xx*.Contoso.msft Properties dialog box.

23. On the View menu in the Active Directory Users And Computers snap-in, click Advanced Features.

24. In the console tree, select Active Directory Users And Computers [Srvdc*xx*.Domain*xx*.Contoso.msft].

25. On the Action menu, click Connect To Domain.

    The Connect To Domain dialog box appears.

26. Click the Browse button.

    The Browse For Domain dialog box appears.

27. Select the Contoso.msft node in the tree, and then click OK.

28. Click OK to close the Connect To Domain dialog box.

29. Expand the Contoso.msft node, and then select the Students node.

30. In the Details pane, double-click Student *xx*.

    The Student *xx* Properties dialog box appears.

31. Open the Published Certificates tab.

    The list of X.509 certificates published to this user account appears.

32. Click OK.

33. In the console tree, select Active Directory Users And Computers [Instructor01.Contoso.msft].

34. On the Action menu, click Connect To Domain.

    The Connect To Domain dialog box appears.

35. Click the Browse button.

    The Browse For Domain dialog box appears.

36. Expand the Contoso.msft node, and then select the Domain*xx*.Contoso.msft node.

37. Click OK.

38. Click OK again to close the Connect To Domain dialog box.

39. Close the Active Directory Users And Computers snap-in.

▶ **Encrypting a folder by using EFS**

1. Open My Computer, and then open the D:\Documents And Settings\Student*xx* folder.

2. Select the My Documents folder.

3. On the File menu, click Properties.

   The My Documents Properties dialog box appears.

4. Click the Advanced button.

   The Advanced Attributes dialog box appears.

5. Select the Encrypt Contents To Secure Data check box, and then click OK.

6. Click OK to close the My Documents Properties dialog box.

   The Confirm Attribute Changes dialog box appears.

7. Select the Apply Changes To This Folder, Subfolders And Files radio button.

8. Click OK.

   The My Documents Properties dialog box appears, and then the Applying Attributes Status message box appears. When the operation is complete, the My Documents Properties dialog box closes.

9. The Student*xx* window appears.

   Notice that the Attributes setting for the selected My Documents folder is Encrypted.

10. Close the Student*xx* window.

Exercise 3
Creating and Using a Security Analysis and Configuration Console

In this exercise, you will create a custom console containing the Security Analysis And Configuration snap-in and the Security Templates snap-in. You will then customize a template and open a new database by using the custom template. You will then analyze the security settings of Srvdc*xx* against the template, and then apply the template's configuration to the security settings of Srvdc*xx*.

▶ **Adding the Security Analysis And Configuration snap-in to a Microsoft Management Console (MMC) console**

1. Log on to the Contoso domain as Student*xx* with a password of "password."

2. Click Start, and then click Run.

3. In the Open drop-down list, type **mmc**.

   An MMC console appears.

4. On the Console menu, click Add/Remove Snap-In.

   The Add/Remove Snap-In dialog box appears.

5. Click the Add button.

   The Add Standalone Snap-In dialog box appears.

6. In the list of available snap-ins, double-click Security Configuration And Analysis and double-click Security Templates.

7. Click the Close button.

   Two snap-ins (Security Configuration And Analysis and Security Templates) have been added to the list on the Standalone tab of the Add/Remove Snap-In dialog box.

8. Click OK.

9. On the Console menu, click Save.

   The Save As dialog box appears.

10. In the File Name text box, type **Security**, and then click the Save button.

▶ **Configuring security by using the Security Template snap-in**

1. Expand the Security Templates node, and then expand the D:\Winnt\Security\Templates node.

   All of the defined templates appear in the console tree.

2. Expand the Securedc node.

   This is an incremental security template typically used after a basic security template is applied. For the purpose of this exercise, this template is sufficient.

3. Expand the Account Policies node, and then select the Password Policy node.

   Password policy settings appear in the Details pane.

4. In the Details pane, double-click Minimum Password Length.

   The Template Security Policy Setting dialog box appears.

5. In the Password Must Be At Least control, change the value to 5 characters, and then click OK.

6. In the console tree, select the securedc node.

7. On the Action menu, click Save As.

   The Save As window appears.

8. In the File Name text box, type **customdc**, and then click the Save button.

9. In the console tree, select the customdc node.

10. On the Action menu, click Set Description.

    The Security Template Description dialog box appears.

11. In the Description text box, type **Custom security template for training**, and then click OK.

12. In the console tree, select the D:\Winnt\Security\Templates node.

    Notice in the Details pane that customdc now has a description associated with it.

13. Read the other template descriptions to become familiar with the templates included with Microsoft Windows 2000 Server.

▶ **Creating a new security database**

1. In the console tree, select the Security Configuration And Analysis node, and then read the text in the Details pane.

2. On the Action menu, click Open Database.

   The Open Database dialog box appears.

3. In the File Name text box, type **Training**, and then click the Open button.

   The Import Template dialog box appears.

4. Select Customdc.inf, and then click the Open button.

   This is the custom template you created in the previous procedure.

▶ **Analyzing current security settings**

In this procedure, you analyze the current settings of Srvdc*xx* against the custom template you created in a previous procedure.

1. In the console tree, verify that the Security Configuration And Analysis node is selected.

2. On the Action menu, click Analyze Computer Now.

   The Perform Analysis dialog box appears, showing the path and name of the error log as D:\Documents and Settings\Student*xx*\Local Settings \Temp\Training.log.

3. Click OK.

   The Analyzing System Security status box appears while various aspects of the security configuration are checked against the template.

4. When the analysis is complete, expand the Security Configuration And Analysis node.

5. Expand the Account Policies node, and then select the Password Policy node.

   In the Details pane, both template settings and the computer's settings are displayed for each policy. Discrepancies appear with a red circle and a white "X" in the center. Consistencies appear with a white circle and a green check mark in the center. If there is no flag or check mark, the security setting is not specified in the template.

6. In the console tree, select the Security Configuration And Analysis node.

7. On the Action menu, click Configure Computer Now.

   The Configure System dialog box appears.

8. Click OK.

   The Configuring Computer Security status box appears while the computer is being configured.

9. On the Action menu, click Analyze Computer Now.

   The Perform Analysis dialog box appears.

10. Click OK.

    The Analyzing System Security status box appears while the system's security is being analyzed.

11. Review the policy settings to verify that the values in the Database Setting column are equivalent to the values in the Computer Setting column.

12. Close the Security snap-in.

    A Microsoft Management Console message box appears.

13. Click the Yes button.

14. If a Save Security Templates dialog box appears, click the Yes button.

Lab 12: Backing Up and Restoring Data

Objectives

After completing this lab, you will be able to

- Use Microsoft Windows Backup to back up files on your hard disk.
- Restore data that has been deleted from your hard disk.

Estimated time to complete this lab: 30 minutes

Exercise 1
Backing Up Files

In this exercise, you will use the Backup wizard to back up files to your hard disk. You will then create a backup job and use Task Scheduler to schedule the backup operation at a later time.

▶ **Creating, running, and verifying a backup job**

1. Log on to the Contoso domain as Student*xx* with a password of "password."

2. Click Start, and then click Run.

    The Run dialog box appears.

3. In the Open drop-down list, type **ntbackup**, and then click OK.

    The Backup - [Untitled] dialog box appears.

4. Read the descriptions appearing for the three options on the Welcome tab, and then click the Backup Wizard button.

    The Backup tab becomes active, and the Backup wizard starts.

5. Click Next.

    The What To Back Up screen appears, prompting you to choose the scope of the backup job.

6. Select the Back Up Selected Files, Drives, Or Network Data radio button, and then click Next.

    The Items To Back Up screen appears, prompting you to select the local and network drives, folders, and files to be backed up.

7. Expand the My Computer node.

8. Select System State. (Do not select the check box to the left of System State.)

    Notice that in the Details pane, the options include Active Directory, Boot Files, Certificate Server, COM+ Class Registration Database, Registry, and Sys Vol.

9. In the left pane, expand and select the C: node. Do not select the check box to the left of the C: drive icon.

10. In the Details pane, select the Boot.ini check box, and then click Next.

    The Where To Store The Backup screen appears.

Note If there is no tape drive connected to your computer, the Backup Media Type drop-down list will be gray because the File option is the only backup media type available.

---

11. In the Backup Media Or File Name text box, type **d:\backup1.bkf**, and then click Next.

    The Completing The Backup Wizard screen appears, showing the details of the backup job to be conducted and allowing you to continue or further configure the job.

12. Click the Advanced button to specify additional backup options.

    The Type Of Backup screen appears.

13. Look at the backup types listed in the Select The Type Of Backup Operation To Perform drop-down list.

14. Verify that Normal is selected.

15. Verify that the Backup Migrated Remote Storage Data check box is cleared.

    This option supports hierarchical storage management (HSM) features in Microsoft Windows 2000 Server.

16. Click Next.

    The How To Back Up screen appears, prompting you to specify whether or not to verify the backed up data after the backup job.

17. Select the Verify Data After Backup check box, and then click Next.

    The Media Options screen appears, prompting you to specify whether to append this backup job to existing media or overwrite existing backup data on the destination media.

18. Select the Replace The Data On The Media With This Backup radio button.

    Notice the Allow Only The Owner And The Administrator Access To The Backup Data And To Any Backups Appended To This Media check box. This option provides greater security because when it is selected, only the backup owner and the administrator can recover a backup job. Make sure this check box is not selected.

19. Click Next.

    The Backup Label screen appears, prompting you to supply a label for the backup job and for the backup media.

    Notice that Windows Backup generates a backup label and media label by using the current date and time.

20. In the Backup Label text box, type **Boot.ini backup set created on** *date* (where *date* is today's date and time).

21. Leave the Media Label text box as is, and then click Next.

    The When To Back Up screen appears, prompting you to choose whether to run the backup job now or schedule the backup job for a later time.

22. Verify that the Now radio button is selected, and then click Next.

    The Completing The Backup Wizard screen appears.

23. Click the Finish button to start the backup job.

    Windows Backup briefly displays the Selection Information dialog box, indicating the estimated amount of data for, and the time to complete, the backup job.

    Then Windows Backup displays the Backup Progress dialog box, providing the status of the backup operation, statistics on estimated and actual amount of data being processed, the time that has elapsed, and the estimated time that remains for the backup operation.

24. When the Backup Progress dialog box indicates the backup is complete, click the Report button.

    Notepad starts and displays the backup report.

    The backup report contains key details about the backup operation, such as the time it started and the number of files backed up.

25. Examine the report, and when you are finished, close Notepad.

26. In the Backup Progress dialog box, click the Close button.

    The Backup - [Untitled] dialog box appears with the Welcome tab active.

▶ **Creating, running, and verifying an unattended backup job**

In this procedure, you create a backup job and use Task Scheduler to schedule a backup operation at a later time.

1. On the Welcome tab, click the Backup Wizard button.

    The Backup wizard appears.

2. Click Next.

    The What To Back Up screen appears, prompting you to choose the scope of the backup job.

3. Select the Back Up Selected Files, Drives, Or Network Data radio button, and then click Next.

    The Items To Back Up screen appears, prompting you to select the local and network drives, folders, and files to be backed up.

4. Expand the My Computer node, expand the C: node, and then select the Inetpub check box.

5. Click Next.

    The Where To Store The Backup screen appears, prompting you to select the destination for your backup data.

6. In the Backup Media Or File Name text box, type **d:\backup2.bkf**, and then click Next.

    The Completing The Backup Wizard screen appears.

7. Click the Advanced button to specify additional backup options.

   The Type Of Backup screen appears, prompting you to select a backup type for this backup job.

8. Verify that Normal is selected.

9. Click Next.

   The How To Back Up screen appears, prompting you to specify whether to verify the backed up data after the backup job.

10. Select the Verify Data After Backup check box, and then click Next.

    The Media Options screen appears, prompting you to specify whether to append this backup job to existing media or overwrite existing backup data on the destination media.

11. Select the Replace The Data On The Media With This Backup radio button.

12. Verify that the Allow Only The Owner And The Administrator Access To The Backup Data And To Any Backups Appended To This Media check box is not selected, and then click Next.

    The Backup Label screen appears, prompting you to supply a label for the backup job and for the backup media.

13. In the Backup Label text box, type **Inetpub backup set created on *date*** (where *date* is today's date and time).

14. Leave the Media Label text box as is, and then click Next.

    The When To Back Up screen appears, prompting you to choose whether to run the backup job now or schedule the backup job for a later time.

15. Select the Later radio button.

    The Set Account Information dialog box appears, prompting you for the password for the Contoso\Student*xx* account. (If the Task Scheduler service is not set to start automatically, you might first see a dialog box asking whether you want to start the Task Scheduler. Click OK, and then the Set Account Information dialog box appears.)

    Because the Task Scheduler service automatically runs applications within the security context of a valid user for the computer or domain, you are prompted for the name and password under which the scheduled backup job will run. For scheduled backup jobs, you should supply a user account with permission to gain access to all the folders and files to be backed up.

16. Verify that Contoso\Student*xx* appears in the Run As text box, and then type **password** in the Password text box and the Confirm Password text box.

17. Click OK.

18. In the Job Name text box, type **Inetpub backup**, and then click the Set Schedule button.

    The Schedule Job dialog box appears, prompting you to select the start time and schedule options for the backup job.

19. In the Schedule Task drop-down list, select Daily, and in the Start Time control, enter a time five minutes from the present time.

20. Click the Advanced button.

    The Advanced Schedule Options dialog box appears.

21. Select the End Date check box, and in the End Date drop-down list, select tomorrow's date, and then click OK.

22. In the Schedule Job dialog box, click OK.

23. On the When To Back Up screen, click Next.

    The Completing The Backup Wizard screen appears, displaying the options and settings you selected for this backup job.

24. Click the Finish button.

    The Backup - [Untitled] dialog box appears with the Welcome tab active.

25. Close the Backup - [Untitled] dialog box.

    When it is time for the backup job to begin, Windows Backup starts and performs the requested backup operation.

26. Start Microsoft Windows Explorer, and verify that Backup2.bkf is added to the D: drive at the appropriate time.

▶   **Viewing and configuring tasks**

In this procedure, you view and then delete the scheduled backup task.

1. Click Start, point to Programs, point to Accessories, point to System Tools, and then click Scheduled Tasks.

   The Scheduled Tasks window appears. Notice that the Inetpub Backup task appears.

2. Double-click Inetpub Backup.

   The Inetpub Backup dialog box appears.

   Notice the text in the Run text box. This is the ntbackup command with the parameters created by the Backup wizard.

Tip If you need to stop a service, such as Microsoft Certificate Services, before running a backup routine, you can create a batch file (.CMD or .BAT) that stops the service, runs the backup routine, and then restarts the service. From a command prompt, type **net stop "certificate services"** to stop Certificate Services. Type **net start "certificate services"** to restart Certificate Services.

---

3. Open the Schedule tab.

   Notice that this is the schedule you created by using the Backup wizard.

4. Click OK to close the Inetpub Backup dialog box.

5. On the File menu, click Delete.

   The Confirm File Delete message box appears, asking whether you want to delete the scheduled task.

6. Click the Yes button.

7. Close the Scheduled Tasks window.

Exercise 2
Restoring Data

In this exercise, you will delete the Boot.ini file and then run a restore routine to restore the Boot.ini file.

▶ **Deleting critical data**

In this procedure, you will intentionally delete Boot.ini. Typically, deleting critical files is an accident or a result of hardware failure.

1. Open Windows Explorer, and then select the C: node.

    The right pane contains the folders and files on the C: drive.

2. Select the Boot.ini file.

3. On the File menu, click Delete.

    A Confirm File Delete message box appears, asking if you are sure you want to delete this file.

4. Click the Yes button.

    The Boot.ini file is now gone. While you could recover it from the Recycle Bin, you will use the restore program in the next procedure to recover the file backed up in Exercise 1.

▶ **Restoring critical data**

1. In Windows Explorer, select the D: node.

2. Double-click the Backup1.bkf file.

    The Windows Backup window appears.

3. Click the Restore Wizard button.

    The Restore wizard appears.

4. Click Next.

    The What To Restore screen appears, prompting you to select the backup media from which you wish to restore files.

5. In the What To Restore box, expand the first backup job you created in Exercise 1.

    Notice that C: appears as the first folder in the backup file. Windows Backup creates a separate backup set for each volume backed up. All folders and files backed up from a single volume appear under the drive letter for the volume.

6. Expand the C: node.

    The Backup File Name dialog box appears with D:\Backup1.bkf in the Catalog Backup File text box.

    If D:\Backup2.bkf appears, change the name to D:\Backup1.bkf.

7. Click OK.

8. When you are returned to the What To Restore screen, select the C: node (not the check box).

    Boot.ini appears in the Name column.

9. In the Name column, select the Boot.ini check box, and then click Next.

    The Completing The Restore Wizard screen appears, prompting you to start the restore operation and use the default restore settings.

10. Click the Advanced button.

    The Where To Restore screen appears, prompting you for a target location to restore files.

11. Click the Restore Files To drop-down list to review the restore location options.

12. Verify that Original Location is selected, and then click Next.

13. The How To Restore screen appears, prompting you to specify how to process duplicate files during the restore job.

14. Verify that the Do Not Replace The File On My Disk (Recommended) radio button is selected, and then click Next.

15. The Advanced Restore Options screen appears, prompting you to select security options for the restore job.

16. Verify that the Restore Security check box is selected, clear the Restore Junction Points, Not The Folders And File Data They Reference check box, and then click Next.

    The Completing The Restore Wizard screen appears, displaying a summary of the restore options you selected.

17. Click the Finish button to begin the restore process.

    The Enter Backup File Name dialog box appears, prompting you to supply or verify the name of the backup file that contains the folders and files to be restored.

18. Verify that D:\Backup1.bkf is entered in the Restore From Backup File text box, and then click OK.

    The Restore Progress dialog box appears, providing the status of the restore operation, statistics on estimated and actual amount of data being processed, the time that has elapsed, and the estimated time that remains for the restore operation.

19. When the Restore Progress dialog box indicates that the restore is complete, click the Report button.

    Notepad starts and displays the report. Notice that the details about the restore operation are appended to the backup log. This provides a centralized location from which to view all status information for this backup and restore operation.

20. Examine the report, and then close Notepad.

21. Close the Restore Progress dialog box.

22. Close Windows Backup.

23. In Windows Explorer, select the C: node. Notice that Boot.ini has been restored.

Lab 13: Implementing Disk Quotas and Monitoring Performance

Objectives

After completing this lab, you will be able to

- Implement disk quotas.
- Use the System Monitor snap-in to monitor system performance.

Estimated time to complete this lab: 35 minutes

Exercise 1
Implementing Disk Quotas

In this exercise, you will configure default quota management settings to limit the amount of data users can store on drive D: of Srvdc*xx*. Drive D: contains the HomeDirs share that includes the folder you created for user John Smith to store his files. Next you will configure a custom quota setting for a user account. You will increase the amount of data the user may store on the D: drive. Finally you will turn off quota management for the D: drive.

▶ **Configuring quota management settings**

1. Log on to the Contoso domain as Student*xx* with a password of "password."

2. Open My Computer, and then open the Properties dialog box for the D: drive.

3. Open the Quota tab.

   Notice that disk quotas are disabled by default.

4. Select the Enable Quota Management check box.

   The other options on the Quota tab are now active.

5. Select the Limit Disk Space To radio button.

6. Type **10** in the Limit Disk Space To text box, and then type **6** in the Set Warning Level To text box.

7. Change the unit sizes to MB for both text boxes, and then click the Apply button.

   A Disk Quota message box appears, warning you that the volume will be rescanned to update disk usage statistics if you enable quotas.

8. Click OK to enable disk quotas.

▶ **Creating a custom quota setting for the John Smith user account**

1. On the Quota tab, click the Quota Entries button.

   The Quota Entries For New Volume (D:) dialog box appears. Notice that the user accounts you created, the NT Authority\System and the Builtin\Administrators group, are listed. The user accounts you created are added because all three accounts (Jane Doe, John Smith, and Bob Train) own files on the volume.

2. Double-click John Smith.

   The Quota Settings For John Smith (John_Smith@Contoso.msft) dialog box appears.

3. Increase the amount of data that John Smith can store on drive D: by changing the value in the Limit Disk Space To text box to 20 MB and the value in the Set Warning Level To text box to 16 MB.

4. Click OK.

5. Close the Quota Entries For New Volume (D:) dialog box.

▶ **Disabling quota management**

1. On the Quota tab, clear the Enable Quota Management check box.

   Notice that the remaining options on the Quota tab are now disabled.

2. Click the Apply button.

   A Disk Quota message box appears, warning that if you disable quotas, the volume will be rescanned if you enable them later.

3. Click OK.

4. Click OK again to close the New Volume (D:) Properties dialog box.

5. Close the My Computer window.

Exercise 2
Monitoring System Performance

In this exercise, you will create a chart in the System Monitor snap-in to display performance data in real time. Real-time charts provide a quick overview of the current performance of your system. You will also create and view a log of processor activity. Logs gather and record data to a file over a period of time and are useful in predicting long-term trends or in troubleshooting short-term problems.

▶ **Configuring the chart**

1. Click Start, point to Programs, point to Administrative Tools, and then click Performance.

   The Performance MMC console appears.

2. In the console tree, select the System Monitor node.

3. Click the Add button (the plus sign) on the toolbar.

   The Add Counters dialog box appears.

4. Verify that Processor appears in the Performance Object drop-down list.

5. In the Select Counters From List box, select %DPC Time, and then click the Explain button.

   A new window appears below the Add Counters dialog box. The window contains an explanation of the %DPC Time counter.

6. Click each of the counters for the Processor object, and read the counter definition for each.

7. Select the All Counters radio button to select all counters for the Processor object.

8. Click the Add button, and then click the Close button.

   A graph appears displaying the processor's real-time activities.

▶ **Generating and viewing data**

1. Click Start, point to Programs, point to Accessories, point to Games, and then click Pinball.

   The 3D Pinball For Windows - Space Cadet window appears.

2. Play one ball (and only one ball) of Pinball. To shoot a ball, press the spacebar for a few seconds and then release it.

3. Close Pinball, and switch to Performance Monitor.

Note If you get a message that data collection is taking longer than expected, click OK to close the message box.

4. In the list of counters displayed in the lower part of your screen, select the % Processor Time counter, and notice the changing Average value.

Tip While looking at the activity of several counters on the Performance Monitor display, it may be difficult to distinguish a given counter's activity. In order to highlight the activity of a particular counter on the Performance Monitor display, select the counter name, and then press CTRL+H. Once you have turned on highlighting, you can select a different counter name to highlight its activity.

---

5. Start and minimize the Active Directory Users And Computers snap-in.

   Notice the activity in the System Monitor chart.

6. Close the Active Directory Users And Computers snap-in.

   Notice the activity in the System Monitor chart.

▶ **Creating a counter log**

1. Expand the Performance Logs And Alerts node, and then select the Counter Logs node.

   A sample log appears in the Details pane.

2. On the Action menu, click New Log Settings.

   The New Log Settings dialog box appears.

3. In the Name text box, type **Performance data**, and then click OK.

   The Performance Data dialog box appears with the General tab active.

4. In the Current Log File Name text box, verify that D:\PerfLogs\Performance_data_000001.blg appears.

5. Click the Add button.

   The Select Counters dialog box appears.

6. Select the All Counters radio button, click the Add button, and then click the Close button.

   The counters for the Performance object are added to the Counters list.

7. In the Interval text box, type **1** so that data is sampled every second.

8. Open the Log Files tab.

9. In the Comment text box, type **Sample performance data**, and then open the Schedule tab.

   A Performance Data message box appears, asking whether to create the D:\PerfLogs folder.

10. Click the Yes button.

11. In the Start Log group of the Schedule tab, verify that the At radio button is selected, and then schedule a start time for two minutes from now.

12. In the Stop Log group, select the After radio button, and then set the service to stop logging in two minutes.

13. Click OK.

The Performance Data counter is added to the Details pane.

▶ **Viewing a counter log**

1. After the counter log has stopped running, select the System Monitor node in the console tree.

Note You can determine whether a counter log is running by the color of its icon. If the icon is green, the counter is running. If it is red, the counter is stopped. Note, however, that if the list of counter logs does not appear to be refreshing itself dynamically, you should refresh the screen manually in order to determine the latest status of a counter log.

2. On the toolbar, click the View Log File Data button.

The Select Log File dialog box appears.

3. Navigate to D:\PerfLogs, select the Performance_data_000001.blg file, and then click the Open button.

4. On the toolbar, click the Add button.

The Add Counters dialog box appears. Note that Processor is the only performance object available in the Performance Object drop-down list. Only the counters that you defined in the counter log are available in the Add Counters dialog box.

5. Select the All Counters radio button, click the Add button, and then click the Close button.

Note If you receive a warning that the counter is already active, click OK to close the message box.

The logged counter activity appears in the System Monitor graph.

6. Close the Performance console.

Lab 14: Configuring Microsoft Windows 2000 Application Servers

Objectives

After completing this lab, you will be able to

- Configure and access the Administration Web site.
- Configure the Telnet service.
- Install and configure Terminal Services and Terminal Services Licensing.

Estimated time to complete this lab: 45 minutes

Exercise 1
Accessing the Administration Web Site

In this exercise, you will use the Internet Information Services snap-in to configure the Administration Web site. You will configure access to this sensitive area of the Web server and then open the Internet Information Services Web page to test access to the site.

▶ **Configuring the Administration Web site with the Internet Information Services snap-in**

1. Log on to the Contoso domain as Student*xx* with a password of "password."

2. Click Start, point to Programs, point to Administrative Tools, and then click Internet Services Manager.

   The Internet Information Services snap-in appears.

3. In the console tree, expand the * srvdc*xx* node.

   Four containers appear under the * srvdc*xx* node: Default FTP Site, Default Web Site, Administration Web Site, and Default SMTP Virtual Server.

4. Expand the Administration Web Site node.

   Notice that two virtual directories appear: IISAdmin and IISHelp.

5. Select the Administration Web Site node.

6. On the Action menu, click Properties.

   The Administration Web Site Properties dialog box appears.

7. With the Web Site tab active, record the TCP Port value appearing in the TCP Port text box. (Note that the port value will vary between 2000 and 9999.)

   _____

8. In the Active Log format drop-down list, verify that W3C Extended Log File Format appears, and then click the Properties button.

   The Extended Logging Properties dialog box appears. Notice that the log file is stored in the %WinDir%\System32\LogFiles folder, which is equivalent to %SystemRoot%\System32\LogFiles.

9. Open the Extended Properties tab.

10. In the Extended Logging Options list, select the Process Accounting check box.

11. Click OK.

12. In the Administration Web Site Properties dialog box, open the Directory Security tab.

13. In the Anonymous Access And Authentication Control section, click the Edit button.

   The Authentication Methods dialog box appears.

14. Select the Digest Authentication For Windows Domain Servers check box.

Note If the Digest Authentication For Windows Domain Servers check box is disabled, select the Integrated Windows Authentication check box and go to Step 16.

An IIS WWW Configuration message box appears, stating that only Windows 2000 domain accounts can be used and that passwords will be stored as encrypted cleartext.

15. Click the Yes button.

This provides additional security in your Microsoft Windows 2000 domain. You will be using only Windows 2000 domain user accounts to access the Administration Web site.

16. Click OK to close the Authentication Methods dialog box.

17. On the Directory Security tab of the Administration Web Site Properties dialog box, click the Edit button in the IP Address And Domain Name Restrictions section.

The IP Address And Domain Name Restrictions dialog box appears.

Notice that the Denied Access radio button is selected and that only the local loopback address 127.0.0.1 is granted access to this area.

18. Select the Granted Access radio button so that you can access the Administration Web site from any computer in your training network. (This step is performed for training purposes only.)

19. Click OK.

20. Click OK again to close the Administration Web Site Properties dialog box.

The Inheritance Overrides dialog box appears and explains that the IISAdmin child node defines the value of the IP Address Restrictions property. You will override the currently configured value in favor of the value you configured for the Administration Web Site node.

21. In the Child Nodes list, select IISHelp, and then click OK.

22. Close the Internet Information Services snap-in.

▶ **Accessing the Administration Web site from the Internet Information Services Web page**

Note The <tcp_port> variable in this procedure must be replaced with the value you obtained in the previous procedure.

1. Open Microsoft Internet Explorer and go to *http://srvdcxx:<tcp_port>*.

A Microsoft Internet Explorer message box appears, stating that you are not running a secure connection for Web-based administration. This means that while authentication information between the browser and the Administration Web site is secure, data transmission after the connection is established is not secure.

2. Click OK.

   The Internet Information Services home page appears.

3. Explore the three Web sites appearing in the main window of the interface. Notice how the links in the left frame relate to the navigation controls in the Internet Information Services interface.

4. Close Internet Explorer.

▶ **Configuring Secure Sockets Layer (SSL) access to the Administration Web site**

In this procedure, you apply the SSL protocol to the Administration Web site to establish secure communication when operating on this site. To do this, you will issue your own server certificate by using Microsoft Certificate Services.

1. Open the Internet Information Services snap-in, and then expand the * srvdc*xx* node in the console tree.

2. Open the Properties dialog box for the Administration Web Site node, and then open the Directory Security tab.

3. In the Secure Communications section, click the Server Certificate button.

   The Welcome To The Web Server Certificate wizard appears.

4. Read the information on this screen, and then click Next.

   The Server Certificate screen appears.

5. Verify that the Create A New Certificate radio button is selected, and then click Next.

   The Delayed Or Immediate Request screen appears.

6. Select the Send The Request Immediately To An Online Certification Authority radio button, and then click Next.

   The Name And Security Settings screen appears.

   Notice that the default name given to this certificate is Administration Web Site and that the bit length is set to 512 bits.

7. Click Next.

   The Organization Information screen appears.

8. In the Organization drop-down list, type **Contoso Corporation**, and in the Organizational Unit drop-down list, type **Contoso Press**.

9. Click Next.

   The Your Site's Common Name screen appears.

10. In the Common Name text box, type **srvdc*xx*.domain*xx*.contoso.msft**, and then click Next.

    The Geographical Information screen appears.

11. Do not change the value in the Country/Region drop-down list.

12. In the State/Province drop-down list, type **Washington**, and in the City/Locality drop-down list, type **Seattle**.

13. Click Next.

    The Choose A Certification Authority screen appears.

14. In the Certification Authorities drop-down list, select Srvdc*xx*.Domain*xx*.Contoso.msft\Domain*xx* CA.

15. Click Next.

    The Certificate Request Submission screen appears.

16. Read the summary information on this screen, and then click Next.

    After a few moments, the Completing The Web Server Certificate Wizard screen appears.

17. Click the Finish button.

    In the Administration Web Site Properties dialog box, notice that in the Secure Communications section of the screen, the View Certificate button and the Edit button are now available.

18. In the Secure Communications section, click the Edit button.

    The Secure Communications dialog box appears.

19. Select the Require Secure Channel (SSL) check box.

20. Verify that the Ignore Client Certificates radio button is selected, and then click OK.

21. Open the Web Site tab.

22. In the SSL Port text box, type **5000**, and then click OK.

23. Close the Internet Information Services snap-in.

▶ **Testing access to the secured Administration Web site**

In this procedure, you test access to the Administration Web site now that a server certificate and SSL have been configured for the site.

1. Open Internet Explorer, and go to *http://srvdcxx:<tcp_port>*.

   A message screen appears, stating that the page must be viewed over a secure channel.

2. In the Address drop-down list, type
   https://srvdc*xx*.domain*xx*.contoso.msft:5000, and then press ENTER.
   The 5000 value is the SSL port value you entered on the Web Site tab.

   A Security Alert message box appears, stating that you are about to view information over a secure connection.

3. Select the In The Future, Do Not Show This Warning check box, and then click OK.

   The Enter Network Password dialog box appears.

4. In the User Name text box, type **studentxx**; in the Password text box, type **password**; and in the Domain text box, type **contoso**.

5. Select the Save This Password In Your Password List check box, and then click OK.

   The Internet Information Services Web page appears. Notice that there is a lock icon in the bottom right corner of the status bar.

6. Place the mouse pointer on top of the lock icon.

   Notice that a tip states: "SSL secured (56 Bit)." 128-bit encryption is available from the Secure Communications dialog box for the properties of the site. In the previous procedure, you configured SSL for the connection, but you did not require 128-bit encryption.

7. Double-click the lock icon.

   The Certificate dialog box appears.

8. Review the information on the tabs of the Certificate dialog box.

   From the Certificate dialog box you can run the Certificate Import wizard to copy certificate information from the local computer to a certificate store.

9. Click OK.

10. Close Internet Explorer.

Exercise 2
Configuring and Connecting to the Telnet Service

In this exercise, you will configure the Telnet service and then connect to the Telnet service and verify the connection.

▶ **Enabling and configuring the Telnet service**

1. Log on to the Contoso domain as Student*xx* with a password of "password."

2. Click Start, point to Programs, point to Administrative Tools, and then click Services.

   The Services snap-in appears.

3. In the Details pane, double-click Telnet.

   The Telnet Properties (Local Computer) dialog box appears.

4. In the Startup Type drop-down list, select Automatic.

5. In the Service Status section, click the Start button.

   A Service Control status box appears briefly as the Telnet service starts.

6. Click OK to close the Telnet Properties (Local Computer) dialog box.

7. Close the Services snap-in.

▶ **Using the Microsoft Telnet Client**

In this procedure, you connect to the Telnet service from the Microsoft Telnet Client. For this procedure, the Telnet client and the Telnet server are on the same computer, although they would normally be separate computers.

1. Click Start, and then click Run.

   The Run dialog box appears.

2. In the Open drop-down list, type **telnet**, and then click OK.

   The Microsoft Telnet command prompt appears.

3. Type **help** or **?** to see a list of available commands.

   A list of supported commands appears.

4. Type **open srvdc*xx***.

   A Welcome To Microsoft Telnet Server message appears.

Note You can use abbreviations for Telnet commands. For example, o srvdc01 is equivalent to open srvdc01.

---

5. Any commands that you can run from the command line on Srvdc*xx* can be run from the Telnet shell.

6. Leave the Telnet session active while you complete the next procedure.

▶   **Running the Telnet Server Administration tool**

In this procedure, you monitor the Telnet service for Telnet client connections and then disconnect the connected Telnet client by using the Telnet Server Administrator.

1. Click Start, and then click Run.

    The Run dialog box appears.

2. In the Open drop-down list, type **tlntadmn**, and then click OK.

    The Telnet Server Admin utility command window appears.

3. Type **1** to list the current users, and then press ENTER.

    Statistics on the Student*xx* user appear.

4. Type **2** to terminate a user session, and then press ENTER.

    A message appears, instructing you to enter a user's session ID.

5. Type **1**, which is the session ID of the connected user, and then press ENTER.

    A list of command options reappears.

6. Return to the Microsoft Telnet client window.

    Notice that the connection with the host was lost.

7. Press any key to continue.

    You are returned to the Microsoft Telnet Client command prompt.

8. Type **q** or **quit**, and then press ENTER to close the Microsoft Telnet Client command window.

9. Return to the Telnet Server Administrator command window.

10. Type **0**, and then press ENTER to close Telnet Server Administrator.

Exercise 3
Installing and Configuring Terminal Services and Terminal Services Licensing

In this exercise, you will install Terminal Services and Terminal Services Licensing.

▶ **Installing Terminal Services in Remote Administration mode**

1. Log on to the Contoso domain as Student*xx* with a password of "password."

2. Open the Add/Remove Programs utility in Control Panel, and then launch the Windows Components wizard.

3. Select the Terminal Services check box, and then click Next.

   The Terminal Services Setup screen appears.

4. Read the information on the screen, verify that the Remote Administration Mode radio button is selected, and then click Next.

   The Configuring Components screen appears as Windows 2000 configures and installs components.

5. If the Files Needed dialog box appears, verify that \\Instructor01\Windist appears in the Copy Files From drop-down list, and then click OK.

   After a few minutes, the Completing The Windows Components Wizard screen appears.

6. Click the Finish button.

   A System Settings Change message box appears, informing you that you must restart the computer before the settings will take effect.

7. Close the Add/Remove Programs window, and then close Control Panel.

8. In the System Settings Change message box, click the Yes button to restart the computer.

9. When the computer restarts, log on to the Contoso domain as Student*xx* with a password of "password."

▶ **Installing Terminal Services Licensing**

Note In a production environment, it is advisable to install licensing services on a computer that is not also running Terminal Services in Application Server mode.

1. Open the Add/Remove Programs utility in Control Panel, and then launch the Windows Components wizard.

2. Select the Terminal Services Licensing check box, and then click Next.

   The Terminal Services Setup screen appears.

3. Select the Application Server Mode radio button, and then click Next.

   The next Terminal Services Setup screen appears.

4. Verify that the Permissions Compatible With Windows 2000 Users radio button is selected, and then click Next.

   The next Terminal Services Setup screen appears, stating that Windows 2000 Administration Tools might function improperly if Application Server mode is enabled.

5. Click Next.

   The Terminal Services Licensing Setup screen appears.

6. Select the Your Entire Enterprise radio button.

   Notice that the license server database will be stored in D:\Winnt\System32\LServer.

7. Click Next.

   The Configuring Components screen appears as Windows 2000 configures and installs components.

8. If the Files Needed dialog box appears, verify that \\Instructor01\Windist appears in the Copy Files From drop-down list, and then click OK.

   After a few minutes, the Completing The Windows Components Wizard screen appears.

9. Click the Finish button.

   A System Settings Change message box appears, informing you that you must restart the computer before the settings will take effect.

10. Close the Add/Remove Programs window, and then close Control Panel.

11. In the System Settings Change message box, click the Yes button to restart the computer.

12. When the computer restarts, log on to the Contoso domain as Student*xx* with a password of "password."

13. Click Start, point to Programs, point to Administrative Tools, and then click Terminal Services Licensing.

    The Terminal Services Licensing snap-in appears, and the Terminal Services License Manager status box appears as Terminal Services are located. Once Srvdc*xx* is found, it appears in the Details pane with a status of Not Activated.

14. In the Details pane, select Srvdc*xx*.

15. On the Action menu, click Activate Server.

    The Licensing wizard appears.

16. Click Next.

    The Connection Method screen appears.

17. In the Connection Method drop-down list, select Telephone, and then click Next.

    The Country/Region Selection screen appears.

18. Select a country, and then click Next.

    The License Server Activation screen appears.

19. Without entering a license server ID, click Next.

    A Licensing Wizard message box appears, stating that the license server ID entered is not valid or was not entered.

20. Click OK.

21. On the License Server Activation screen, click the Cancel button.

22. Close the Terminal Services Licensing snap-in.

    The Terminal Services Licensing component is installed, and you will be able to use Terminal Services in Application Server mode for 90 days. Before 90 days have passed, you must activate the server by using the Terminal Services Licensing snap-in and information provided to you by Microsoft Corporation.

▶ **Preparing an application for Terminal Services Application Server mode**

In this procedure, you uninstall the Windows 2000 Administration Tools and then reinstall them to ensure that they will run properly from a terminal session.

1. Open the Add/Remove Programs utility in Control Panel.

2. In the Currently Installed Programs list, select Windows 2000 Administration Tools, and then click the Remove button.

    An Add/Remove Programs message box appears, asking if you want to remove the Windows 2000 Administration Tools from your computer.

3. Click the Yes button.

    A Windows Installer status box appears, and then a Windows 2000 Administration Tools status box appears as the tools are removed.

    Notice that the Add/Remove Programs window no longer contains the Windows 2000 Administration Tools.

4. Close the Add/Remove Programs window, and then close Control Panel.

5. Click Start, and then click Run.

    The Run dialog box appears.

6. In the Open drop-down list, type **adminpak.msi**.

    Adminpak.msi is located in the D:\Winnt\System32 folder, which is in the search path. Therefore, there is no need to type the path to this Microsoft installer file.

7. Click OK.

    The Windows 2000 Administration Tools Setup wizard appears.

8. Click Next.

   The Installation Progress screen appears as the administrative tools are installed. When the installation is complete, the Completing The Windows 2000 Administration Tools Setup Wizard screen appears.

9. Click the Finish button.

   The additional administrative tools have been re-installed under Administrative Tools.

Scenario A: Setting Up New User Accounts

Objectives

After completing this scenario, you will be able to

- Create user accounts and user groups.
- Set up the appropriate permissions for the new users.

Scenario

Your organization is hiring 20 temporary users to work on a specific project that will last only a few months. The users will need to access some network resources, such as servers and printers, but they should not be able to access many of the resources that the full-time employees can access. You want to be able to administer these user accounts as efficiently as possible but maintain the security necessary to protect your organization while granting the users the necessary access rights.

1. Which tool would you use to create the necessary user accounts and user group?

   _____

2. What steps would you take to create the user accounts and user group?

   _____

   _____

   _____

   _____

3. How would you limit access to certain network resources while granting access to other resources?

   _____

   _____

   _____

Scenario B: Setting Up Dfs

Objectives

After completing this scenario, you will be able to

- Set up and configure a Dfs root.
- Set up and configure a Dfs link.

Scenario

Your organization includes five geographical locations that are linked together in a common domain namespace. Each location is fairly independent and maintains much of its own accounting-related data on servers within that geographical region. Corporate headquarters needs to be able to access this data regularly, but individual users at headquarters are finding that it is a complicated process to access the various servers. As a result, you are setting up Dfs to simplify access for these users.

1. How would you set up the Dfs structure to support this data access?

   _____

   _____

   _____

   _____

2. How would you create any necessary Dfs roots or Dfs links?

   _____

   _____

   _____

3. How would the Dfs structure be maintained?

   _____

   _____

   _____

   _____

   _____

Scenario C: Configuring a DHCP Scope

Objectives

After completing this scenario, you will be able to

- Add and configure a DHCP scope.
- Exclude certain IP addresses from that scope.
- Create client reservations for specific resources.

Scenario

A set of about 30 users and their computers are being added to your organization. Your network is configured to automatically assign IP addressing information to any new computers added to the system. However, the current DHCP scopes are not enough to support the number of new computers that will be added to the network. As a result, you must configure a new DHCP scope to support the new users. However, some of the IP addresses available to your organization have been assigned to specific resources, and some resources need to be assigned the same IP address every time.

1. How would you configure the DHCP scope to support the new computers?

_____

_____

_____

_____

_____

_____

2. How would you exclude IP addresses from distribution?

_____

_____

_____

3. How would you set up client reservations?

_____

_____

_____

Scenario D: Monitoring System Performance

Objectives

After completing this scenario, you will be able to

- Monitor your system's performance.
- Create counter logs to monitor performance.

Scenario

You have received complaints from several users that they often have difficulty connecting to a computer running Windows 2000 Server between 1:00 p.m. and 3:00 p.m. You decide to monitor system performance on that computer between those hours.

1. What tools should you use to monitor system performance?

   _____

   _____

2. How would you collect real-time data about the computer?

   _____

   _____

   _____

   _____

   _____

3. How would you set up logging to collect data every day between 1:00 p.m. and 3:00 p.m.?

   _____

   _____

   _____

4. How would you view the logs that you created?

   _____

   _____

   _____